SEVEN DAYS

SEVEN DAYS

AUTHENTIC CONVERSATIONS AND RELATIONSHIPS
THAT CHANGED MY LIFE AND MY FATHER'S DEATH

DIAN REID

iUniverse, Inc.
Bloomington

Seven Days
Authentic conversations and relationships that
changed my life and my father's death

iUniverse books may be ordered through booksellers or by contacting:

iUniverse
1663 Liberty Drive
Bloomington, IN 47403
www.iuniverse.com
1-800-Authors (1-800-288-4677)

Because of the dynamic nature of the Internet, any web addresses or links contained in this book may have changed since publication and may no longer be valid. The views expressed in this work are solely those of the author and do not necessarily reflect the views of the publisher, and the publisher hereby disclaims any responsibility for them.

Any people depicted in stock imagery provided by Thinkstock are models, and such images are being used for illustrative purposes only.
Certain stock imagery © Thinkstock.

ISBN: 978-1-4759-7488-1 (sc)
ISBN: 978-1-4759-7489-8 (ebk)

Printed in the United States of America

iUniverse rev. date: 01/31/2013

Contents

Acknowledgements

First and foremost, I thank my father for his strength in words, love, and honesty during his final months on this earth. Without his candidness and authenticity there would be no story for me to tell.

To my partner in love and life, Erin, I am always grateful for her continued support. It's through her patience and encouragement I gained strength to see this book through to its publication.

I thank Reese* for her compassion and love during my father's illness and after the end of our relationship. I'm grateful for our continued friendship, as well as her willingness to allow me to share the difficult details of our relationship, at least from my side.

To my family, I am ever grateful for your strength and support, both at my father's side during his final days, as well as by my side as I tell this story.

I set out in October 2006 to write this book, and nearly two years later I barely had a thousand words written, let alone a thirty-thousand-word manuscript. Thank you to my dear friend Michelle Farish for introducing me to my life coach, Kristi Pallino. Kristi was fierce in her commitment to both this book and me; without her dedication, this book might still be swirling around in the chambers of my memory.

The sixth draft was the first draft I was willing to let anyone's eyes see. I handed a copy of that draft to several people, asking for different types of feedback from each. Without the feedback from these wonderful people, my story would not have evolved into what you're about to read. Thank you, from the depths of my soul, Lisa Mae Brunson, Jenifer Maxwel, Caroline Nemec, Alessa Carlino, and Jill Christy.

I am indebted to Crissy Jancic, because without her, this would be a bumbling mess of words with no structure and barely a thread to tie each part of this story together. Without her guidance on structure and content, this book would not be what you have in your hands today.

Once the manuscript was fully written, multiple drafts edited, poked and prodded at, Alessa Carlino again stepped in to help, and coached me to the proverbial finish line. Without her this book might still be sitting in a "drafts" folder on my Macbook.

I hold immense gratitude for my editor, Jan Howarth, for keeping the integrity of the story and my voice in telling it throughout the editing process. Her expertise and guidance were invaluable in this book reaching your hands.

And finally, a heartfelt tip of my hat to Daniel De La Rosa for making my vision of the cover of this book come to life. This is how I will always remember my father: mustached and smiling in a plaid flannel shirt, holding on to the love of his life.

---

*Author's Note: Some names have been changed either by request or to protect their anonymity.

For my father—I inherited your patience and perseverance, and alas, this book is born.

Preface

A week after my sixteenth birthday, my father said six words to me that changed my life.

He pulled up to the front of the home I lived in at the time, met me in the driveway, and said: "It's your mother. She's dead, Dian."

Four gunshots. One of them hit the wall between her bedroom and my two-and-a-half-year-old brother's room. One hit the floor. And two hit my mother in the stomach.

She died in minutes. Actually, I read that on the death certificate months afterward. My grandparents thought I was too young to know any of the details. Even at sixteen, I knew that, had I been older, they still wouldn't have talked any more about the incident to me.

I had no one to talk to. My grandmother was guilt stricken because she'd said no when her daughter told her she wanted to leave her boyfriend, Steven, and move back into her childhood home. My grandfather believed my mother got what she deserved; after all, she hadn't been strong enough to leave him sooner. My uncle was heartbroken at losing his only sister, and learned to keep it all inside—when you're heartbroken, no one else wants to hear about it. My father was stunned at losing his former wife, the mother of his only child, and looked to God for a reason. And me? I looked around and tried to make sense of it all. *Would anything have changed if my grandmother had said yes? Did my mother really deserve her death because she was too weak to leave her boyfriend? Should I keep my heartache to myself because no one wants to hear about it? Should I ask God what to do?*

When my mother died, I lost her completely. But this story is not about her death.

I spent the next decade and a half wondering when and how my father would die. Not dreading his death, but wanting to know the "when" so I could control the "how." At least, how I would deal with it.

My mother died unexpectedly, abruptly; my father gave me time to adjust. Time to say good-bye.

He gave me seven days.

A Patient History

Gerald Clark Reid. Also known as Jerry Reid, father, brother, and friend. Sometimes known as "JR," but mostly he was just Jerry. Five feet, eleven inches tall. Dark brown hair, hazel eyes. Olive-toned skin on his farmer's tanned arms, and Scottish—and Irish-white paste on all the rest of his unexposed skin. Sturdy and strong. No chiseled muscles, and still he was a single-employee moving company when I needed him to be. His days off were few and far between, as were his self-employment paychecks toward the end of his career.

He was most comfortable in Levi's and a paint-splattered, white T-shirt beneath a plaid, long-sleeved button-up, the sleeves rolled halfway up his arms. My father loved his tan work boots and didn't believe in steel toes until he couldn't find boots without them. He did crossword puzzles in pen and completed every Sunday *LA Times* Daily Crossword for as long as I can remember. He completed the *NY Times* Crossword every chance he got, and it was his dream to one day finish a crossword from *The Times*—the famous London newspaper.

He had an awful 1967 full-size Chevy truck, which we'd dubbed "The Green Monster." It was a lime-ish green (or at least it used to be), and the bed overflowed with tools and ladders and tarps and spare tires mixed in with rubber belts and hoses, boxes and fast food remnants, paint, brushes, thinner, and rollers. The truck's original paintjob had mostly chipped away, and it was difficult to see where the once-white stripe down the side ended and the rust began.

On the weekend days I rode to work with him. He'd stop at the 7-Eleven right around the corner from his apartment and pick up a Pepsi (always in a glass bottle until they switched solely to plastic), an apple Danish, and a Snickers bar. That was breakfast. Lunch was usually a Carl's Jr. value meal with a Sprite (always a Sprite), and, occasionally, he ventured out to Del Taco, Burger King, or McDonald's. Dinner was sometimes Kraft Mac and Cheese or Campbell's Chunky beef soup, or a frozen dinner, usually of the chicken pot pie variety.

In November 2004, my father had his gall bladder removed. Later that month he was told it had been filled with cancerous cells and that they believed they'd gotten it all, but he should undergo chemotherapy just to be on the safe side. In December, he started chemotherapy. By July the next year, he had finished chemotherapy and been given a clean bill of health. In September 2005, he had a blockage in his liver, which was only discovered after six weeks of tests, but the cause was undetermined, and according to the doctors (or just my father's version of their words), there was no reason to believe it was cancer related.

In October 2005, the blockage was confirmed to be cancer related.

Conversation with my father never provided me with the level of detail I would've gotten directly from the doctors. It wasn't that he didn't listen, or that the whole process didn't interest him, or even that he didn't understand it all. It was that his memory wasn't what it used to be. While the doctors spoke, he understood everything they said, but when he tried to repeat what the treatment would be, there were things he left out. Things like "rare cancer." Things like "terminal." And things like "twenty percent chance of living five more years."

Then again, it was cancer. Maybe he *couldn't* remember everything exactly and just gave me what he *could* remember. Maybe he *didn't* understand it all and gave me only what he *did* understand. Or maybe he was just as scared of the words as I was.

Given the fear likely swimming around in his head, I couldn't rely on my father to give information freely, regardless of whether or not he understood that information. And with fear swimming around in my own head, I was afraid to ask him for more than the ambiguous recounts of the doctors' diagnoses he was able to give me—partially because I felt it in my gut, and partially because I didn't want to know what I already *knew*. But I asked my father anyway. I asked him if he had terminal cancer. He simply reported a statistic the doctors had given him: "Twenty percent of people with this kind of cancer live out five years. Best case scenario."

Five years? Twenty percent? Is that out of twenty million people or one million? Are there four million people that have this cancer and live five years and then just drop dead? Is that how this works? I barraged my father with question after question, almost not waiting for an answer.

He responded to all of them, simply, calmly as ever: "No, Dian, that's not how it works. This type of cancer is *rare*. Maybe one thousand people in the United States."

Five years . . . twenty percent . . . five years . . . twenty percent . . . The words sprinted aimlessly through my brain. "And how long have you been sick?" I asked. He replied matter-of-factly, "Well this is a part of the cancer they found last year."

Last year. *You mean last Thanksgiving day when you called me to tell me they took out your gall bladder and they found it cancer ridden but thought they got it all out? You mean that cancer? The cancer you got a year's worth of chemotherapy for and then got a clean fucking bill of health after? That cancer? That's the one that's giving you five years to live? So one year down, four to go? And that's best-case scenario? Best case. Best. That's bullshit. Bull. Fucking. Shit.*

Of course, I could bring myself to say none of that. I stood silent, paralyzed by a cancer that didn't even inhabit my own body. Meanwhile, my mind raced.

"They" couldn't possibly be right about this. This was LA. There were a lot of doctors, and some were bound to make mistakes. So what if they went to UCLA med school? So what if these doctors knew what they were talking about?

I resolved to fight this preposterous cancer with my father and prove those incompetent doctors wrong.

But first my father started to act sick. *Get* sick. *Show* sick. The sickness settled in. The cancer sat down for its meals. The meals became longer. I learned that, between September and November of 2005, my father lost sixty pounds. He went from 225 pounds to just 165. The latter was his weight in high school when he played tennis six hours a day. He would lose ten more pounds over the next month, after which I stopped asking about his weight.

In November 2005, my father was back in the hospital after feeling faint and having low blood points or whatever it's called when Coumadin thins the blood too much. In all the time I spent listening to doctors and my father talk about his blood levels for this and that—for rising and falling, for Vitamin K, for Coumadin, for heart surgery, for cancer, for liver blockage, for gall bladder removal—you'd think I'd know some of the terms by then, by now. But I didn't; I don't. I stood in the corridor of the Westwood Veterans Affairs Hospital that November and asked one of the many doctors tending to my father, "So how close is he?"

Doctors get a look on their faces that actors attempt to recreate—to mimic—when it's time to give bad news. I've seen it on *Grey's Anatomy* and *ER*, and even when they come close, it always looks like acting, like mockery, like they're *trying* to make the face.

Her soft eyes and slightly raised brow, her pressed lips, her ever-so-subtle and slow intake of breath and subsequent pause before speaking, her blatant and direct eye contact, the slight flare of her nostrils as she began to breathe out again and words rode the conveyer belt out of her mouth: "In my experience . . ."

First of all, let me say that I don't give a shit about your experience, just tell me about my goddamn father.

". . . patients who return with your father's frequency . . ."

And, secondly, I don't give a shit about other patients or the frequency of their fucking visits.

". . . and with the type of complications he's having, tend to be toward the end of their life cycles."

The end of what? Are you fucking kidding me? He's supposed to have four more fucking years!

"I can't say for sure that your father has a specific amount of time left, but I would venture to say that he's closer to the end of his life cycle . . ."

I had insult after insult ready to spew at her about what a huge mistake she'd made. That she couldn't possibly be right about my father or his condition. That she must've gotten her medical degree from a Cracker Jack box. That she looked too young to know what she was talking about, and I'd like to talk to a *real* doctor up in this joint.

Instead, I held my tongue, knowing she didn't need her script. Unlike Hollywood actors, this doctor—this woman—with one simple look, told me what I needed to know: my father was dying, and quickly.

In early December 2005, my father appointed me his power of attorney and signed DNR documents: do not resuscitate.

CHRISTMAS NIGHT 2005

I pulled up to the house and parked in the driveway. A driveway I'd parked in hundreds of times. Thousands, probably. It used to be my grandparents' house. When my grandmother died, it became just my grandfather's house. Then when he died, I inherited half of it. I chose not to live there with all the painful memories of lives and deaths and everything in between. My father was inside, living out the rest of his days in avoidance of the flight of stairs to reach his own rented room across town. I sat in the car after I turned off the engine and prepared myself for the rest of the night. I closed my eyes and took a deep breath. Then another. In. Out. In. Out. Shoulders back, head held high, I opened my eyes. I turned off the headlights and opened the car door. My heart beat faster as I stood up and walked toward the house. I opened the door.

I was late to pick my father up, but he didn't mention it. He sat, sunken on the couch, and I wondered if was the couch or him that was sunken. A smile came across his face that read: "I don't know how much longer I can hold on." He sat, dressed and resting. He seemed confused. He said he didn't know where his shoes were. I went into the bedroom and retrieved them from the floor next to his bed, where he had asked me to set them the day before. I brought them to him in the living room and placed them near his feet. He put them on. He stood up and steadied himself for the walk to the door. He rested at the dining table before he reached the door. He rested at the door before he stepped outside. He rested at the car before he got inside.

My Honda Accord was low to the ground, and he struggled to get in. His belly had grown from the cancer, and he struggled with the seatbelt. Fluids no longer drained from him properly, so his body didn't get rid of most of the toxins most of us pee out after drinking a glass of water. He always felt full. The doctor told him he had to force himself to drink water, even when it was painful. A sip of water filled him up. He was dehydrated most of the time because he didn't—couldn't—drink enough water.

I made sure his seatbelt was buckled, then took a deep breath and pulled out of the driveway. I drove toward Uncle Johnny's house, thirty miles north. I took the freeway. As I motored along quietly, just maintaining the speed limit, a car swerved right and a large piece of paper flew into my driving path and attached itself to the grill of my car. It blocked my headlights for a few seconds then part of it whipped up to block much of the windshield. I could no longer see clearly in front of me and turned my right blinker on. I began to pull to the side of the road, and my father gasped, a delayed reaction to what had happened. He was slower in his movements and his reactions to everything. His brain didn't respond the way it used to. I pulled off the highway and stopped the car on an off-ramp. I got out of the car. I removed the paper from my headlight, from the windshield, and tossed it aside for someone else to tangle with. I got back in the car, shivered off the cold, and looked over at my father. He said, "It's cold out there." *Yes. Yes, it is.*

My father had been to Johnny's several times, and he knew the way. Or he used to know the way. For our trip, he had directions written down. I exited the freeway and turned according to my father's verbal instructions. I turned right. Then left. Then followed this road until I hit that road. I turned left again. My father confirmed that we were on the right street. He gave me the house number. It didn't match up with the numbers on the houses. He looked confused. I'd not been to Johnny's since he bought his new house. It all looked unfamiliar to me. I asked to see the address he'd written down. He became agitated. He shifted and squirmed, and his pants squeaked against the leather seat. He darted his eyes and moved his head from right to left, as if the sweeping motion would capture new information and make clear his error. I asked if we should call the house to confirm the address. My father did not like this idea and reluctantly searched for his phone. He pressed buttons and held the phone to his ear. There was no sound. I saw that he had not pressed the send button, but I said nothing. The pit in the top of my stomach could not bear to point out his blunder. He pulled the phone away from his ear and looked at it, as if for answers. I suggested he press Send harder. He pressed Send. My father spoke briefly to Johnny's wife, Bertha, and wrote down a new number. My father had scrambled the address and told me the right number. He pressed End. We were on the right street; we just needed to drive farther. We reached the house. I parked. I helped him out of the car. He leaned on the car and rested.

We stood at the front door. I pushed the doorbell. The door swung open. Rick, my father's younger brother, Johnny's older brother, opened the door. Rick's face lit up at his first sight of my father. Shock then flashed over Rick's face. He hadn't seen my father since Thanksgiving. My father's face was gaunt and jaundiced. His eyes were grey and sunken. The brothers hugged. Rick lovingly slapped my father on the back. "It's good to see you, brother." They walked into the living room where my father was greeted by the rest of the family.

For dinner we were served salad, tamales, beans, and rice. Flan and ice cream were served for dessert. It was not what I was used to for Christmas dinner. I prepared a plate with small portions for my father: part of a tamale, a sugar spoonful of beans, and a forkful of rice. He hardly touched any of it. This was his new appetite. He was not bitter about this; he simply accepted it as the reason he'd lost seventy pounds over the last four months. I didn't talk at the dinner table. I sat quietly and listened to others. I took a bite of food and I listened. Took a bite and listened. *Bite. Listen.* When my plate was empty, I took it into the kitchen. Bertha's mother took my empty plate and exchanged it for a plate of flan. I did not want the flan, but I took it. I sat at the table and I took a bite, listened, took a bite until the plate was empty. I had been eating slowly, it seemed. Johnny and Rick had retired to the living room. I walked my father twenty paces from the table to the couch. He sat at one end of the couch, winded. I sat at the other end, closest to Rick and Johnny. Rick, Johnny, and I engaged in conversation while my father sat back and listened. He had no strength to contribute and seemed content to listen.

He sat in silence, in pain, while we talked and talked and talked. We laughed and talked, and every now and then I looked over at my father and his silence just to make sure he was breathing. He was. Rick said something funny. Johnny laughed. I laughed. My father mustered a quiet chuckle. I looked over to make sure he wasn't choking. He was not. I breathed.

Two hours had passed since we had arrived. My father told me he was tired. He needed to go home. We said our good-byes. We walked to the car. I opened the car door for him. He struggled to get in. He struggled with the seatbelt. He did not sleep, but he was quiet. I saw his belly rise and fall over and over on the way home. I saw because I looked at him often. He was breathing, and I was happy about that. He told me he'd had a good time at the dinner party. He told me he enjoyed seeing everyone.

A quiet smile fell over his face. He did not speak the rest of the way home.

At home, I laid out his bedclothes. I tucked him into bed. I kissed his forehead and told him I loved him. I told him Merry Christmas. He smiled. He said good night. He loved me, too. Alone in my car on the way home, I cried and thought to myself, *That was the Last Christmas.*

Day 1

Back and forth, back and forth, my eyes darted from her eyes to the clock on my wrist . . . the clock to her moving lips. The nurse wasn't finished going over everything about my father's outpatient hospice care, but I had an 8:55 p.m. flight to catch. Even with 9/11 five years behind us, I was antsy about getting to the airport two hours before my flight departed. No one got through security quickly anymore, even with no baggage to check and a limp, laptop-less backpack slung over her shoulder. Sweat was dampening my palms as I repeatedly glanced at my wristwatch, silently begging this woman to make this all go away.

My father had been taking liquid morphine every twelve hours. Then when he had breakthrough pain he took a morphine pill. Which would have been fine, except the liquid was for breakthrough pain and the pill was his daily medication to be taken every twelve hours. When he took the liquid, it knocked him silly, rendering him incomprehensive of himself and his surroundings. The liquid also didn't last very long, so breakthrough pain came often. The pills weren't strong enough to fight the breakthrough pain; neither were they fast acting. They only kept him more disoriented when he took another dose of the liquid. It was a vicious cycle he had been keeping himself on, and he needed to be monitored. Which was the reason for the hospice care. He was willing to agree to hospice care, but only if he could stay comfortable at "home."

We'd been going over my father's condition for the better part of two hours, and I could no longer control the anxiety I felt in needing to get the hell out of there. I'd convinced myself that if much more time passed I'd miss the next bus to LAX and, in my irrational mind, miss my flight to serenity. I interrupted the intake nurse to ask how much longer she'd need to go over whatever details she hadn't already given me of my father's expected care, and she told me she was actually just about to finish up. She had only a few documents for me to sign, and I could be on my way if I didn't have any questions to ask. *Yeah, I have a question. Can you fucking fix my father? No? Well then, let me get the fuck out of here.* Add that to the list of unspoken questions and quips I would never dare say aloud. I signed all the necessary documents and was relieved time didn't permit me to stay and ask questions.

Not that I knew which questions to ask anyway. Which was why Vickie was there.

Vickie was my boss by title, friend by virtue. I'd worked either with her or for her for nearly seven years at the time, at the same company. I remember being scared out of my mind when this fiery red head interviewed me for a customer service position. I thought I projected a slick image by acting tough, telling her that what she saw was what she got and that I wouldn't be any different come six months if she hired me. She trusted her gut to tell me I looked horribly tense and uncomfortable, and she hoped I would relax bit, given six months' time. With that, I sank back into my chair like a caricature of myself and sighed a deep breath of relief that I didn't have to pretend I was a perfection-driven hard-ass anymore. That's when the real interview started, a prelude to my nearly eight years with that company.

Over the years we got to know each other, spending many lunch hours chatting about the mundane details in our lives, as well as the glaring differences in our religious and general beliefs about the world. Vickie had a knack for being curious about who I was and what made me tick without being judgmental—something she was far better at than I for the bulk of our friendship. I loved her because she took care of me as if I were her own child, and while our core beliefs about God invariably differed, she never treated me as anything other than human. From Vickie I learned how to be conscious about releasing judgment on people, and for that I will always be grateful. I'll also always be grateful to her for her willingness to share the experience she'd gained working in a nursing home. For several years she had volunteered her time as part of her Christian community service.

With the paperwork signed and me all out of time, Vickie offered to stay with my father and the hospice care nurse to ask the questions she knew I'd want to have answers to, sift through the details she knew I'd want clarified, and gather information on what situations to expect as my father continued dying.

I should stay. I shouldn't want to get out of here so quickly, so badly. Am I really gonna miss my flight if I don't leave right now? I felt guilty for leaving before everything was finalized, but I needed to get on that plane. Sanity was on that plane and where it landed, and I needed the sanity of alone time more than I needed to be there for the questions, the answers, the dying. I needed some sanity outside of Los Angeles.

Fuck sanity! I need Reese. I needed to be with my girlfriend. I needed her comfort, her warmth, her strength, her arms, her skin, her scent. I needed to be 900 miles away from imminent death to get it. Whoever and whatever else I needed, I knew I wouldn't find them by asking more questions about the details of my father's hospice care.

I stared at the traffic and shifted with the bus as it turned right and left and eventually hauled itself up the ramp, onto the 405 freeway and headed south toward LAX airport. I pulled the only book from my backpack, clicked on the personal light above me, and the pages seemed to flip themselves.

My thoughts faded in and out of consciousness, flowing back and forth between the words on the page, a man snoring a few rows behind me, and blackouts of memories attached to my father's old life—the one he used to have, and the one I used to know before he got sick.

A clear Sunday morning in the park watching my father play softball in the sun. A cloudy Saturday afternoon watching my father build a deck on the back of his best friend's house. A chilled Monday night swinging a softball bat and sprinting around the bases, sliding into third while my father watched with glee from the recreation park bleachers. A warm Sunday afternoon of conversation in my apartment on my father's way home from the morning service at his Foursquare Church down the street. Those and countless random days in between drowned in the syrup of "things that will never happen again."

The bus dropped me and my thoughts off to wander the terminals in LAX in search of my flight.

As I walked past the arrival and departure monitors, I saw that my flight had been delayed. "TBD" took the place of a departure time. *Great. Now I feel like an ass for leaving early.* I wanted to feel like crying, but I didn't, so I felt guilty instead and sat down near the gate to wait for an actual departure time to be announced. The incoming flight from wherever it originated—I could never remember or care which city—was delayed due to bad weather, as Reese had warned it might be. Flying didn't bother me as much as it did Reese, but I'd done a lot more of it, having traveled sporadically for business the previous couple of years: Chicago in November for a client presentation, San Francisco in August for a new client rollout, Las Vegas in April for schmoozing, New York in September for training. I had always enjoyed the time on the plane to myself and was still alive to tell about it, so it didn't make sense to me to worry about it. No matter how many flights I'd taken, I'd never thought twice about getting on in the past; this flight was different. I was anxious and restless even as I tried to remain calm. It seemed to me the trying negated the feeling of calm, and my keen observation of this only made it worse.

"Anything to drink?" a flight attendant asked after we uneventfully took off. I'd hardly noticed her standing there. *A beer sounds good,* I thought, but asked for a water instead. Just the thought of digging for my wallet wasn't worth the extra movement. A different flight attendant set my water down on the fold-down tray in front of me, and I stuck my nose back into *Dark Nights of the Soul* by Thomas Moore.

Reese had gotten it for me after my grandfather died in July, but I hadn't started reading it until after I'd scheduled the hospice meeting just a week prior. See, I hadn't struggled to find peace with my eighty-four-year-old grandfather's death. But I did with my father's.

Half pretending, half reading, I thumbed through a few pages, barely taking in any information. My eyes land on:

> There is no loss too great or challenge too
> overwhelming, provided you are anchored
> in your vision and your values, while
> following your destiny.[1]

What the fuck is that supposed to mean? I kept reading, my brain too long in the off position to attempt either answering the question or contemplating the passage any further. A sprinkle of momentary disgust and moving on was the only MO I could muster.

As the flight ascended through the rain and clouds, I became aware of how glad I was that Reese wasn't on the plane with me. Her fingers would have been clenched around mine as wind blew the tiny plane—or maybe it just felt tiny—left and right, and clouds along the way rocked us up and down. For a moment I hoped the plane would go down, and even wondered if I'd get mobile service at that altitude to call Reese and say good-bye. The thought didn't bother me as it meandered through my mind; it fit nicely with the helplessness that had embraced me since I left the hospice meeting. It was almost comforting to think the plane might crash and I wouldn't have to deal with hospice or cancer or any more deaths in my family.

The captain ordered the flight attendants back to their seats until further notice and apologized for having to cancel beverage service. I sat still in my seat, seatbelt securely fastened, and held my cup of ice water, imagining it was a vodka on the rocks. I sipped slowly and wished I could imagine a sad enough orchestra tune as I closed my eyes and the plane went down like the *Titanic* in my head.

In real life, the turbulence subsided rather quickly, and the plane did not go down. Eventually beverage service was reinstated—and was offered free at that. *Thanks for the inconvenience, much appreciated.* "I'll take a Heineken, thank you." Beer half drunk, I continued to read, trying to concentrate through the movement, the noise, and the alcohol tapping on my weak brain cells.

Fewer "WhatTheFuck?!" moments passed through my head as I read, although I'm certain it wasn't with any higher level of understanding. I kept my head down, eyes on the page, fingers flipping from one page to the next—and the next and the next. I hadn't noticed that the flight attendants had picked up my empty beer can and non-alcoholic vodka cup, or folded my tray upright into the seat in front of me. I looked up from my lap and saw the ground rolling by just outside the window. *Seriously, we're on the ground? Shit, that was fast. I wonder if Reese is here? Does she remember I'm coming?* I knew the answer to all of those questions, and still they couldn't help but permeate my mind with unreasonable doubt that something could and would and must go wrong.

I looked for Reese. She saw me first and walked toward me. I thought I felt joy. I walked toward her and hardly contained myself. *Yes, this is joy. It must be. I should be smiling.* I was smiling. I fumbled with the door that led from the tarmac to the inside of the tiny airport, and it nearly smacked me in the face. I was embarrassed and hoped she hadn't seen me. She had. She smiled. I felt flushed, but continued to walk toward her. We were a few feet apart, and I anticipated her warm welcome—a hug, my head buried in her shoulder. Her eyes looked away and her body shifted quickly away from me as I approached. I was confused at her avoidance, and she steered me toward the exit. It dawned on me that we were in her small hometown. I wouldn't get the welcome I wanted.

I did not expect to make out in the middle of her small-town airport. I just wanted a hug. Something—someone familiar—to hold onto. A place to rest my head, even if for only a moment. Not just anyone. I wanted to wrap my arms around *her* and absorb *her* energy. I wanted to take in the faint scent of Calvin Klein Truth on her neck as I brushed my cheek past hers. I wanted to feel the tingle in my spine as her hands met each other around the small of my back. I didn't just want this, I *needed* this—I needed her. *Is it too much to ask? A little human contact when my father is dying?* Maybe it was. I said nothing, and she said nothing. I thought she apologized with her eyes that it wasn't more. I held hope that she would comfort me when we were out of public sight, and I felt sorry for myself for not being stronger.

Undercover in her father's car, masked by falling rain and darkness, she searched the parking lot quickly for spectators. She gave me a quick kiss, but I smelled no perfume and felt no tingle. With a touch of her chilled, wet lips on mine, I felt the fear in her heart of being seen. I took the fear on as my own. My heart raced, and I looked up to be sure no one had seen us.

In the safety of the car Reese held my hand most of the way home, save when she took the bends in the slippery road, which required the ten-and-two-o'clock position. She asked how the hospice care meeting went. I told her what I remembered and I told her I was scared. I told her I didn't know if I should be away from him. I told her I felt guilty. I told her it felt like too much for me . . . that I could crumble at any moment, and I began to sob. It seemed like only a few seconds had passed before we arrived in the driveway with the car still running, words and sobs still draining from my mouth. I wished the drive were longer just so I could be alone with Reese for more than a rainy ride home on rubber tires.

I asked if we should go in, and Reese said she didn't want to rush me. I took a deep breath and told her about my father looking, feeling, being disoriented. I'd already told her that story while the rubber tires were moving, but she said nothing. She closed the space between us and wiped tears from my face. *Am I crying again? I feel like a fucking blubbering idiot.* I stopped talking. Again, I became overwhelmed by emotion, and it all poured out of me as rain beat relentlessly down on the windshield.

Reese's mother couldn't bear the thought of my arriving without freshly baked pumpkin something waiting on the table for me. She'd baked a fresh loaf of pumpkin bread with no nuts, knowing I'd appreciate it. She also knew I would never ask her to make it especially (or at all) just for me. And no matter how late my flight got in, she was determined to stay up and greet me.

Anna waited until she heard the door from the garage into the house crack open before she got up and walked from the living room into the kitchen to greet us. I was surprised to see her walking without a cane. She'd had hip surgery the day before our last visit the month prior and seemed to be recovering well. She used the island in the middle of the kitchen to lean on and came to wrap her arms around me.

Some hugs are polite, some are nonchalant, some are bear hugs, fierce and unfeeling. Anna's that night was the softest, fiercest, most heartfelt hug I'd felt since my father was strong enough to hug me. Her arms transferred strength and dignity into my soul. She whispered into my ear, "I'm so sorry, Dian. I wish it were different circumstances, but I'm glad you could be here with us." And then she held on a little tighter.

We'd shared a few conversations via phone in the year and a half Reese and I had been dating, and I'd met her just once when I'd stayed in her home shortly after her surgery. Her soft, rosy cheeks rarely held anything but a smile, and she'd never spoken an unkind word to or about me, as far as I knew. She just trusted Reese and figured she'd get to know me later, and in the meantime didn't have to know me inside and out to know that she loved me. It was almost strange to feel so loved by this woman who barely knew me, only what her daughter shared of me, only what a few conversations could reveal.

When Anna and I finally did let go of each other, Reese was just returning to the kitchen, having gone to the rear of the house where the bedrooms were. We met her in the hall. Anna went to sit in her La-Z-Boy recliner in the living room to rest for a moment while Reese showed me to my room. As soon as we rounded the corner into the room, she held on to me. Tight, fierce. This was the welcome I'd been waiting for since the airport. I held her, she held me, and I release myself into her arms where nothing else in the world seemed to matter, only the two of us right then, right there—the smell of her hair, her lips, her skin touching mine. And in that moment, nothing else did matter.

Back in the living room, Anna stood up from her chair to say good night just as Reese and I walked in to say the same to her.

Reese's father, Edward, appeared as if from thin air, stealthily and quiet. His sudden entrance into the room scared the crap out of me, and I jumped slightly out of my skin and tried to hold my composure. My momentary state of shock seemed to be lost on him as he marched right up to me and hugged me without saying a word. A warm bear hug that wasn't a manly hug like he wanted me to know he was boss, but a manly hug like he wanted me to know that he cared. It was a quick hug; he'd made his point, and as he released me, he looked at me, held my shoulders at arm's length, and said, "Good to see you, Dian," and continued on to the kitchen. That was Edward's way. A man of few words, and right to his point.

Reese and I didn't sleep in the same bed under Edward and Anna's roof. It wasn't that they didn't approve of our relationship; they were just old fashioned. We weren't married, and until we were, we would sleep in separate beds. That night, I pretended it didn't bother me.

Reese lay with me for a moment under the covers, then got up and tucked me in and kissed my forehead. When she walked out and closed the door behind her, I lay awake thinking, unable to fall immediately asleep.

It struck me square in the chest that I had left my father—abandoned him. Taking slow and shallow breaths, I thought about how I'd left him in the hands of . . . of himself. I'd left him alone, knowing full well he couldn't take care of himself. My father was helpless while I hopped on a plane that took me nearly a thousand miles away so I could try to get away from it all. There was no getting away from anything, though. The "what ifs" began to flow. *What if something happened and I wasn't there? What if he died and I wasn't there? What if he died alone and I could have been there? What if, what if, what if?*

I shook my head, wiped the tears from my face, and replayed in my head my therapist's advice about the bottom line: even if my father died while I'd been in LA, I probably wouldn't have been right by his side anyway. I would have been in my apartment or Reese's, or I'd have been at work, and would have been guilt-ridden about not being with him, regardless. If he died while I was in LA, I might even find a way to feel guiltier than I already did over getting out of town to refresh myself.

That was the whole point. *Refreshing myself.* I knew what I was going back to. I had no false hopes of an extended life for my father. I knew he wasn't going to live or die based on my decision to skip town for a few days. I knew I wasn't escaping the reality of his death; I was simply preparing for it.

And even with all that "understanding," I still felt guilty for being away from him.

I tried to punish myself by staying awake staring at the ceiling all night, but my eyes would not cooperate for more than a few minutes. I drifted off into a dreamless slumber, silent and still, until I heard the creak of the floorboards as Anna walked by with her cane on her way to morning coffee.

I had slept well and woken up with a renewed sense of guilt.

Day 2

Sunlight shone through the top of the bedroom window. Still nestled in bed, I smelled fresh coffee and heard rumblings of homemade breakfast being put on the breakfast nook table in the kitchen, and birds chirping in the bushes just outside my bedroom window.

Teeth brushed and pajamas still on, I sat at the breakfast nook table with glassy eyes, staring out at the holly bush just beyond the bay window in search of those bedroom birds as they invisibly chirped with madness and rustled the shiny leaves. The morning's conversation had thankfully little to do with my father, and more to do with the birds getting drunk from the holly berries and flying into windows along the side of the house.

Breakfast and drunken-bird talk finished, Reese and I went for a walk in the woods behind the house.

It had rained most of the night, leaving the ground damp and the air thick with chilled fog. The ground, the trees, the air smelled fresh and clean, full of life, and far better than the concrete jungle I'd left back in LA. But even in the backwoods it was too uncomfortable for Reese to walk hand in hand with me. Small-town, everybody-knows-everybody northern California was not big-city, nobody-knows-anybody LA. I thought about how I didn't want a romantic walk in the woods, and how I did need her close to me. After the mild reception the night before at the airport, I needed the simple human connection of her hand in mine, but didn't know how to ask for it. I wanted to reach out, but more than that, I wanted her to reach out for me. I stewed, saying nothing, afraid of the conversation that might unfold if words actually left my lips. In an attempt to avoid the brawl in my head, I allowed my thoughts to wander back to my father. *I can't believe I'm here and not with my father. I hope he's okay. I hope he misses me. I hope he doesn't. Wonder if he took his medication right this morning. Wonder how he'll be when the hospice care nurse comes to take care of him today. I can't believe he can't take care of himself. Can't believe he hasn't taken a bath or a shower in more than a week. Can't believe this is my life.*

With the stealth of knives sharpened by ninjas, my thoughts cut from the woes of my father to woes of my own. *I wish she'd just walk closer to me. I'll just stay back so she's not uncomfortable. I'll just stay back so I don't have to talk to her. I'll just stay back so I can be by myself. I'll just stay back.*

Tears welled in the back of my throat, but I remained silent, resolved to not appear in need. As I fought back barely audible sobs, my thoughts resumed, consuming my sanity. *I wish I had the balls to make her hold my hand. Doesn't she know I need her right now? This isn't about* her; *it's about* me. *How can she be so selfish? I need something from her. I need something more. Something more than a walk in the woods that I might as well be taking by myself. God, I feel so pathetic. It's cold and it's almost fucking raining again, and I don't want to fucking walk anymore. I hate myself right now.*

I realized my cadence had slowed and I'd nearly dropped out of Reese's sight, had she bothered to turn around and look for me.

Maybe I should just drop back, completely out of sight. Just slip away into the woods, never to be seen again. Jesus Christ, don't be so fucking dramatic, Dian, you don't actually want to be alone, do you? Don't drop too far back. She'll come looking for you—if she ever turns around. Make sure she can hear that you're back here; rustle some leaves under your feet. Maybe she thinks you just need this time to yourself. Maybe she needs this time for herself. Maybe she'd rather be alone. Maybe I should just stop thinking and say something. It's been too long since we've said anything to each other. I can't speak now; I won't be the one to break this silence.

We walked for an hour or so in near silence, my mind reflecting thoughts like a house of haunted mirrors. Up this narrow dirt path and down that wide one; through weeping trees and wet brush; onto a paved street to traverse back to the house on a different route than the one we'd set out on. Reese pointed out a house with a rainbow flag and said, "Family lives there." We kept to ourselves as we walked past their home.

In the early stages of coming out as a lesbian, I learned that "family" is how many gays and lesbians refer to each other. When a lesbian asks if you're "family," she's not asking if you're a distant cousin or niece; she's asking if you're part of her urban family of lesbians. Christians have their fish; we have our "family."

I pondered the family that lived in the house Reese had pointed out and wondered if they lived in fear of their conservative town the way Reese did. Reese and I walked silently and briskly the rest of the way back to her parents' house, narrowly escaping a whipping of rain by just a few minutes.

The thing about Reese and I. Things hadn't been going all that well between us, even before my father got sick. I couldn't bear to admit it at the time, but she seemed to be pulling away. The more she pulled away, the harder I tried to reel her back in.

I often wondered why I couldn't still be the calm, cool, collected Dian of the beginning of our relationship. Or why I couldn't stand to be without her. Why I couldn't think about things falling apart. Why I couldn't be angry with her. Why I couldn't speak my mind. Why I feared her reactions. Why I feared the words—the rage—that would escape my mouth, my soul, if I actually let go. *Why, why, why?*

It was no use asking why; I was never going to answer any of those questions.

When my father got sick, I sensed Reese come back to me a little. Maybe she felt obligated to stay with me until the hardship passed. Maybe she didn't want to kick me while I was down. Maybe she actually thought we could work things out. Whatever her reasons, at least it never felt as if she was doing me a favor. Her genuine love and attraction kept her emotions real for me, at least for a while. And still, something—her desire to *stay* with me after my father had died, I suppose—was missing. But I didn't care about her reasons for staying or how long she would; it just felt nice that she hadn't left yet.

As our relationship grew from hanging out to becoming girlfriends to avoiding the conversation about moving in together, I lost the original "plan" of our beginning: summer fun—let's just see where this goes. I wanted so badly to be the romantic story that worked out like a fairytale right from the beginning . . . the one that persevered through thick and thin, regardless of the separating paths we were actually on. But the truth was, our relationship didn't stand a chance, even from the beginning. And certainly not after my father's death. How could I have known that then, though?

I had a phone session scheduled with Kate at 11:00 am. I'd gone back to therapy the day after hearing "twenty percent chance" from my father. The session that morning was a near replica of the one we'd had the week prior, the difference being the details I shared of my father's outpatient hospice care induction.

He could get up and walk from the bedroom to the bathroom, from the bathroom to the kitchen, from the kitchen to the living room, and from the living room to the bedroom. He just had to take breaks in between. If he wanted to go outside, he could probably muster the energy to get there, but he'd have to rest before he came back.

The problem was that I wanted to be there in case he couldn't do something—anything. I wanted to be in control of something that I had no control over. That was the reality that I didn't want to see. *I think it's getting harder to breathe.*

But, I told Kate, what I wanted *more* of at the time was to get the hell out of hospice. As my father sat limp on the couch, barely able to put a coherent sentence together, I felt my heart rip right out of my chest . . . separate itself from the rest of my body, blood dripping on the floor in the form of tears from my eyes as I watched my father literally deteriorate right in front of me. *Am I breathing at all?*

As my conversation with Kate continued, she had to coax me into breathing deeply. "Breathe in deep, Dian. Long . . . slow . . . deep breaths."

When she spoke, she often reminded me of my mother. Not in the actual sound of her voice, but in the soft vibration, the care-giver's tone, the sometimes shallow rasp that would calm me in an instant, the motherly ambiance she created with her energy, and the way it all melted together and sang from her mouth. She reminded me of the ever-elusive simpler times when a mother's soothing voice might actually help.

The breaths Kate guided me through, coupled with her calming voice, finally coaxed me into recognition that I absolutely must be away from my father . . . that I needed the time for myself . . . that my sanity required this time so that, when I returned, I could be fully present with my father and give him the attention he deserved.

The deep breaths helped me subscribe to the idea that I needed to be somewhere away from my father's situation, with someone I felt alive with. That even though leaving him broke my heart, it was necessary to the well-being of both of us. And the last thing I wanted was to resent my father while he lay on his deathbed for the fact that I couldn't catch a break I had absolute control over.

I hung up the phone breathing more calmly and feeling better than when I'd picked it up to call her. Almost immediately, my cell phone rang.

The intake coordinator at the hospice care facility. She had called my father earlier that morning to set up his first home appointment with the nurse to have her administer his medication and give him a bath if he felt up for it. He had wanted no part of it. He had become agitated and confused. He'd insisted that he wouldn't be up to seeing anyone once he returned from his doctor appointment later that afternoon. She urged me to contact my father and talk him into letting the nurse come by as scheduled.

I called my father. There were a number of things that ran through my head when he didn't pick up the phone—that he was asleep or otherwise engaged and simply didn't hear the phone; that he heard the phone, tried to answer it, and didn't get there in time to pick up the receiver; that he purposely didn't answer the phone, thinking it was hospice care calling again; that he'd fallen and lay hurt and abandoned in an empty house in pain; that he'd fallen simply, eternally asleep.

Unable to bear the thought of any further possibilities— and in an attempt to ward off a panic attack in case something horrible had actually happened—I chose to believe that either his hearing had failed him or he wasn't quick enough to get to the phone in time.

A phone call to Vickie revealed that she had stopped by the house earlier that morning to drop off a pillbox for my father, as she'd promised. He thought the visit was unannounced, even though it had been a planned visit they had discussed at the hospice care meeting. She said he seemed a little out of it, but she chalked it up to the fact that it was early in the morning. After I got off the phone with Vickie, I called the house again and got no answer.

I looked at the clock. 12:45 pm. Suddenly it hit me that his doctor appointment was at 2:00. *He's getting ready for his appointment! Thank God! That's why he's not answering the phone—he probably didn't even hear it ring.* My father took nearly a full hour to slowly get ready and leave the house. Carolyn was a dear friend of my father's, a member of the church he belonged to, and the wife of the pastor of that church. She would be picking my father up at 1:30, so if anything happened, she would call me immediately. The timeline seemed believable so I breathed an audible, nervous sigh of relief to myself and sat down on the bed.

Just as I made these revelations and filed them away in my head, Reese came into the room. There had been a mix-up about the timing of lunch with her aunt and uncle, and it had been moved up. We needed to leave right away.

I got dressed frantically and was ready to leave as the family headed for the door. I ran back into the bedroom for my cell phone and saw that it was nearly dead from all the morning's long-distance conversations. I plugged it in and left it on the windowsill to charge until later that evening.

We had lunch with Reese's family. We decided on the way back to the house to pick up dinner at the market. We decided to drop Reese's parents off and go to the store, without going inside to check my phone. We went to the store for dinner steaks and potatoes. We made two more stops on the way home, at an auto parts store and a retirement home. I purchased and installed new windshield wipers in the rain while I waited for Reese to visit with her grandmother. We drove home. I checked the windowsill for my phone. I saw a blinking voicemail light.

Two messages. Both were missed calls from a restricted number. *Oh my God. Something happened to my father.* My heart raced as I mistook shallow breaths for deep ones in an attempt to calm myself down. *Nothing to worry about, Dian, everything's fine. It's fine. It is fine, right?* I took an actual deep breath and nervously dialed into my voicemail.

An annoying, soft computer voice pretending to care addressed me, "Press the pound key to listen to voicemail. Please enter your password. You have two new messages. One message marked urgent." My heart sank and my hands shook. "Press one to listen to new messages." I pressed one. I listened.

"Hi, Dian, this is Carolyn Grissom. Can you please give me a call as soon as you get this message? My number is wah-wah-wah." I hung up the phone, dialed her number, and listened to the phone ring. After the initial quick hello, she asked if I'd spoken to my uncle Rick yet. "No. No, I haven't talked to Rick." "Okay, well, your father seems to have had a stroke, and he's in intensive care over here at Holy Cross Hospital. Where are you?" "I'm in northern California." "I see." *How is he?* I wanted to ask if he was alive, but all I could get out was, "Is he . . . okay?" "He doesn't look so good . . ."

When Carolyn had arrived to pick up my father for his doctor appointment at 1:30, he had seemed confused and disoriented. He didn't know what time it was and seemed to have forgotten about the appointment altogether. He was dressed in week-long-couch-ridden sweats when she showed up, so he went into the bedroom to put street clothes on. When he came out, he wore his sweatpants over his jeans. He said he was cold. He also had trouble using his left hand and arm, and walked into furniture and walls that were on his left. Carolyn thought this behavior might be indicative of a stroke and remained focused on getting my father to the hospital. She helped him to her car and drove him to his appointment. Her instinct may have saved his life—for the time being—and certainly saved my sanity.

After hearing Carolyn's version of my father's situation, the nurse spoke with other nurses and doctors and made an immediate decision to have him transferred to an emergency room. The Veterans Affairs facility where my father had his appointments was an outpatient facility and was not equipped to handle his current condition.

My father's veteran's insurance allowed for treatment by the nearest VA hospital. If that hospital could not take him due to overcrowding, he was allowed to be admitted to the nearest emergency room, whether public or private. And if this happened, the insurance would still cover 100 percent.

The VA hospital in Westwood did not have a bed available. The VA outpatient facility arranged to immediately transfer my father to Providence Holy Cross Medical Center in nearby Mission Hills, and Carolyn followed the ambulance. She stayed with my father until Rick arrived several hours later. My father was stable, but in critical condition, and that's all she knew. After I hung up with Carolyn, I immediately called Rick.

"It doesn't look good, Dian. You'd better get here quick."

The next couple of hours were a blur. Somewhere between my sobbing and explaining, and sobbing some more, Reese got me a flight back to LA. Due to circumstances beyond our control, the only option I had was the first flight in the morning, which left at six.

We ate dinner in near silence . . . brief words of sympathy, then small talk for the rest of the evening.

I felt sick to my stomach. *I must be a horrible daughter.*

Alone in a bed meant for two. On any other trip, I wouldn't have minded the loneliness, the traditional values, or respecting the rules of a home I was a guest in.

But on that night I felt lonely and pathetic. I felt sorry for myself for what felt like the first time (but it must've been the hundredth time) since I found out my father was terminal. He was nearly twenty years younger than either of Reese's parents, and I resented both of them for being alive at all.

I had visions of storming into Reese's bedroom shouting that I didn't care what rules I was breaking. Visions of having a Xena-like confrontation with her parents, in which I would slay them like dragons and ride off into the sunset with Reese behind me on my white unicorn.

Hearing Anna's cane and footsteps down the hall, I snapped out of it and thought to myself, *When you have the cancer then you can feel sorry for yourself, Dian. Put your sword and unicorns away, shut up about your goddamn loneliness, and just fucking deal with this.*

I thought about how frail my father had looked when I left him the day before. The trouble he had understanding what was happening around him. There was a look of shame in his eyes that, I imagine, can only come from knowing what your mind used to be capable of. My father—this man who never bothered with pencils for crosswords—would never meet his goal of finishing a London *Times* crossword. I sighed deeply, feeling a raspy ache at the back of my throat and tears well in my eyes.

Just then, Reese peeked her head around the bedroom door. Without saying a word, she scooted into bed next to me and held me, stroked my hair, wiped the tears from my face. I wanted to lie with her all night, to fall asleep in her arms, for her to dissolve my pain with her touch, her kiss, her voice. What I wanted did not matter if I couldn't speak it. I remained silent as she lay with me until I fell asleep, then slipped away quietly to her own room.

Day 3

The day began feeling *more* than any other day. More clouds. More thoughts. More guilt. More responsibility. More burden. More rain than I knew what to do with. So I just sat in the car and let Reese drive me to the airport.

As the plane touched down at LAX, I looked out the window and saw no clouds. Blue sky. Sunshine.

But I wasn't fooled. The storm would catch LA soon enough.

Vickie picked me up outside the baggage claim I had no use for and drove me on the 405 freeway north towards Mission Hills.

"Are you ready to let go?" she asked.

Anger and hurt started as a tiny lump in my throat and swelled into a giant lump of sadness and loss. I kept them all at bay beyond the back of my tongue as I tried to form words to answer her question. What was the answer?

Was it: *I feel cheated.* No, *I'm not goddamn ready to let go!*

Or: *What the fuck is the matter with you, asking me a question like that? Let go. Let go? Are you fucking kidding me about letting go? No, I'm not fucking ready!*

But I said: "Of course I'm ready to let go; I have no choice."

"Are you ready to tell him it's okay for *him* to let go?"

How am I supposed to tell him it's okay for him to let go? I don't want him to suffer, but how do I tell him it's okay to give up? That it's okay to . . . to just let go?

Silence spoke the single word I was unable to say: *no.*

My father wanted to be the parent in my life who didn't leave his daughter without parents. He wanted to be a father who had thirty more years with his daughter.

I wanted my father to be here, to go to my softball games and cheer all of us on; to come over on Sundays to talk about baseball and avoid politics and other uncomfortable topics; to share holidays and birthdays and random Tuesday evenings with me; to be a father to his daughter.

If everything happens for a reason, shouldn't I just let it happen?

I didn't want him to endure any more pain. I'd watched him enough times, in enough pain—simply to put shoes on, then need to catch his breath before being able to stand up.

Silence had said her peace, and now it was my turn. "I don't want him to suffer anymore," I told Vickie. I knew it was the right answer, and part of me even felt good saying it. Meanwhile, my two-year-old self began a temper tantrum in my mind, kicking and screaming, begging: *No, Daddy, please don't go! Daddy no! Nooooo, Daddy, noooooo!* Kick. Scream. Kick.

Vickie let me have my silent tears, my silent temper tantrum, and drove ahead without saying another word. As my internal tantrum subsided, I heard myself say aloud again, "I don't want him to suffer anymore."

I followed Vickie as she walked into the hospital and found the information desk.

"Which way to Gerald Reid in ICU?" she asked.

"Room 216. There are already two people visiting him, and we have a two-person limit in the ICU . . ."

Within a split second, white rage lit my heart, my lungs, my throat on fire. Just before I could scream, *Get the fuck out of my way—I'm going to see my father!* the nurse continued her sentence to say she could let me through, as long as I sent one person back. She saved me an inferno of embarrassment by dousing my rage with her soft, quick words. I was stunned into silence and simply continued to listen as she pointed the way to my father.

Uncle Rick and Carolyn were in the room. As soon as I walked in, Carolyn nodded, smiled, and went back to the waiting room without a word.

I don't remember what the room in the ICU looked like, but I'll never forget the sight of my father when I walked in. Gray stubbled face. Jaundiced skin. Feeding tube slithering like a snake from his mouth. An octopus of heart and pulse monitors attached to every limb. IV attached like a viper's fangs to the back of his hand. And that look on his face that said, "Well, look what I've gone and done now."

My father was great at taking the blame for things he had no control over. He shrugged his shoulders as best he could lying in a hospital bed, and tried to give a "ta-da" smile.

I took his hand in mine, mindful of the snakes connected to various parts of his hand. I sat silent with him for twenty minutes before the nurse came in and told us that the staff needed to change my father's medications and give him his daily sponge bath. We had to find something else to do for thirty minutes.

Over cafeteria breakfast—which wasn't as bad as people make out hospital food to be—Rick and I avoided conversation about my father until we were nearly finished. Rick asked a question about my father's plans for burial, and I fought through the familiar, strangled feeling in my throat to share what I knew. He had no plot purchased in any cemetery, and he would be fine with being buried for free in a Veteran cemetery, based on the last conversation we'd had about it. My father never intended to be a burden, neither physically nor financially, on his family, even in the preparations for his death. Rick and I would need to talk to Johnny to discuss splitting the cost of the funeral and burial my father deserved.

Unable to get myself to dive into more conversation about the aftermath of my father's cancer and imminent death, I searched for a clock on the wall as an excuse to head back to the ICU. Fifteen minutes had barely passed, and the waiting room would have to do.

On the way back through the halls we walked past a hysterical woman outside the ICU waiting room. She was in tears, sobbing into the red phone attached to the inside of waiting room wall by the door. "I don't know if he's going to make it, he's lost a lot of blood, a lot of blood . . . both his arms and three ribs are broken . . . internal bleeding, and he's still unconscious . . ."

Probably an accident. So glad I'm not her.

Or was I?

At least that man she's here for has a chance at life. At least she has hope. I have no hope. Not the real kind, anyway.

Embarrassed over my judgments against this woman and whomever she was hoping would pull through, I dropped my eyes to the floor and silently wished the woman's hysterical crying out of my presence. I wanted to lash out at her for falling apart right there in front of me, with no regard for my grief for my father. I wanted to scream at her, tell her to shut the fuck up, that we're all trying to hold ourselves together and she had no business feeling her feelings right out in the open for all of us to tap into.

I cannot fall apart. I cannot fall apart. I cannot fall apart. Not yet . . .

Deb and her husband Jon came to visit my father, and his eyes lit up. They had all been friends for nearly thirty years. I left the three of them alone. I didn't need to hear the deathbed conversation between my father and his best friends.

Rick and I went back to the waiting room, where the rest of my father's visitors congregated. No hysterical woman was in sight, just a palpable pity from my father's visitors that made my stomach turn. It reminded me of my mother's cremation—though I hadn't actually watched it take place—and of my grandmother's ashes being placed in the niche with my mother's, almost thirteen years later.

I was sure the people in that room saw a daughter whose mother had been murdered, a granddaughter who had found her grandmother dead on the bathroom floor. Most of them refused to make eye contact with me, I assumed for fear of catching the heartbreak I was obviously enduring, as if it were a virus.

I listened silently to their conversations while my own internal monologue rambled on.

I bet they're glad to be them and not me. I bet they're all grateful for their husbands, their wives, their children they get to go home to tonight. They're probably going to call their mothers, their fathers, their living mentors tonight just to say thank you for still being alive. They're going to hug their children and tell them they love them. And then I bet they're going to pray for me. Fuck them. And fuck their prayers. Prayers will not fix my father.

Pastor Ken (my father always referred to him as Pastor Ken or Pastor, but never just Ken) and his wife, Carolyn, sat in the waiting room with the others.

Pastor Ken spoke of my father's love of cheeseburgers and Sprite for breakfast, lunch, and dinner, and surmised that when he got to heaven, my father would probably be offered an endless supply of Sprite for his good deeds on Earth.

I quietly wondered about heaven—the possibilities of its existence, and why he believed my father was destined to retire there. With cheeseburgers and Sprite, no less.

———～ⁿⁿ◦◦◦✦◦◦◦ⁿⁿ———

So I could take a break from the ICU, Deb and Jon invited me to lunch at a restaurant down the street from the hospital. I must've gone back and forth fifty times in my head over whether or not it was okay to leave my father for an hour. When I finally walked out of the hospital, I realized it hadn't even occurred to me to tell the nurses where I was going or how to reach me in case of an emergency. Another thing to feel guilty about.

Deb and Jon and I settled into a booth with our salads and iced tea while folks who had survived the years my father would never make it to were on their way to early-bird dinners.

My father's friendship with Deb and Jon was living evidence of his card-carrying liberal days, and while I had been around to witness the tail end of them, it was in the role of daughter, not friend, and there was much that I hadn't been privy to.

Jon asked how my father felt about my sexuality. I felt my skin grow conscious of my surroundings, and wondered if people around us heard the question. I acted as if I didn't care what anyone thought about me, but it made my skin crawl to think someone might overhear our conversation. I took a sip of ice water, and words flowed as if I'd thought them up myself.

My father had told me he'd always wondered what his reaction would be if I told him I was gay. He'd thought about the possibilities, and based on his faith in the church and God, didn't want to think *that* of me. He could barely stomach the words *gay* or *lesbian*, and to think his daughter was one of *them* made his heart break, he'd told me. I knew my father didn't approve, and even still I never felt as if his love for me changed. I always said that our relationship never changed, but that came to be a blanket I wore over the truth; in reality's light, the open acknowledgement of my sexuality altered everything about our relationship.

My father came to my house after church every Sunday and went to most of my evening softball games during the week. He became friends with my first girlfriend, Carla, and when we broke up, he was genuinely sad for me. Still, he was hopeful I'd see that the life I'd "chosen" was too difficult and that I might attempt what he thought of as a "normal" relationship. Hell, at times I even thought heterosexuality was "normal," but then the general consensus before 1492 was that the world was flat. I'm normal; I'm just not heterosexual.

Part of my father's thought process was that he didn't want to see me suffer. He saw how people treated gays and lesbians and didn't want his daughter to bear the burdens of that treatment. I didn't see it as suffering; I just wanted to be myself. In all the years I watched my father as I grew up, I never saw him try to be something or someone he wasn't. He sometimes made apologies for not making enough money, for not being a better father, or husband, or friend, but he never apologized for being himself. And because of this, I knew I needed to be *my*self, to stand firm in what I know to be true about myself, and not change who I am because people didn't understand or like it, or because it might make for a hard life. It may have taken time, but people no longer believe the world is flat.

Jon asked if I knew when my father changed from a liberal to a conservative Christian man, and I knew exactly: it was the day my mother died. Some people are born into the Christian faith, while others have a life-altering experience that moves them toward a new or renewed faith. My father was the latter. He needed a reason to have faith in God, and my mother's death sent him to the church, seeking answers. He needed to know that her death meant something. He needed to make sense of the chaos that had become our lives, and turning to God and faith was how he did that.

My parents divorced when I was two years old, and my father never stopped loving my mother. He moved on with relationships and life, but never remarried. They raised me in separate homes, but together in spirit. I saw him nearly every weekend and lived with my mother during the week. In the fourteen years between their divorce and her death, I never saw or heard them fight. Not once.

After her death, I was shocked to find out that my parents didn't get along for years after their divorce, and wondered how that was possible. They had followed a common adult ritual of shielding a child from the arguments of a failed marriage, and I believe myself to be the better for it.

Jon looked across the table at me and said, "Adulthood is overrated."

As we drove back to the hospital, I thought about Vickie's words earlier that morning on letting go. I expected the beads of sweat to return to my palms, my heart to pound with fear, and my lungs to keep my breaths short and useless. Instead, I found myself in a state of peace and calm. A warm glow of energy flowed through my body, and I became so sedate I nearly fell asleep. I was aware of my surroundings, as well as the fact that I was in a dreamlike state, almost as if I'd been slipped a mickey at lunch, as I sank deep into the backseat and became one with Deb's car. My skin morphed into soft fabric, and my veins filled with foam. And then, as quickly as it had come about, the moment passed and I had skin for skin, blood in my veins, flesh on my bones, and life present in front of me, waiting to be lived. *It's time to let you go, Dad. And for you to let me go.*

When I came back to my father's room, he was sleeping.

I thought of how, just four months before, I had taken a ten-day vacation to Germany and needed someone to care for my animals while I was gone. I had friends who lived close by who were happy to do it, but I asked my father instead. The trip from his house to mine was close to twelve miles—which, in LA traffic, translates to at least thirty minutes each way. At the time, the cause of his liver blockage hadn't been attributed to terminal cancer (or cancer of any kind, for that matter). He spent most of his days fatigued from walking and working, and had trouble getting up and down the stairs to his bedroom. My apartment offered him an elevator from the parking garage to the second floor. The cupboards held healthy food (though I'm sure he still made plenty of trips to every fast food joint in the neighborhood), more space than just a fourteen-by-fourteen bedroom in disarray, as well as two cats who would rub up against his legs, his arms, his hands and demand love with enthusiastic meows every time he walked in the door.

Shortly after my trip, a friend of my father's asked him if it had been hard on him taking care of my cats since he was tired most of the time and my apartment was so far from his house. With a sheepish grin he'd said, "It's nice to be needed."

I hadn't noticed my father wake up. His eyes were changing from hazel to gray, which made them look blue. *Circle of life.* I tried to keep my lip from quivering, my voice from cracking. I was marginally successful.

Summoning the strength and peace I'd felt as a part of the backseat of Deb's car, I told him that it was okay for him to let go; that he didn't have to hold on for me; that I'd miss him, but I'd be okay without him; that he was a good father and I loved him; that it was time for him to go home.

As the words came out of my mouth, I couldn't be sure which ones were truth and which were lies. I let them flow all the same. Tears filled my father's eyes and spilled down his cheeks, and he reached out his hand for mine. With my hand in his, he squeezed quickly and gently, with what was surely all his might, and nodded his head in agreement.

Looking deep into my father's eyes, searching for the courage to say my last peace, I recalled taking my father to the VA outpatient care facility for a weekly checkup. When I picked him up, something hadn't been right with him: he'd seemed overly fatigued and his skin was an abnormal shade of gray jaundice, both cases more acute than usual at the time. He told me he hadn't had the energy for the past few days to go for his prescribed daily short walk around the block. He'd crawled into my car, and I'd driven as fast as I could while trying hide the panic attack slowly rising in my chest.

Once in the VA outpatient facility, my father was quickly hooked up to an IV for nutrients by one attendant while another took vital signs and small blood samples. His heart rate was extremely low and gave cause for concern. Enough to send him via ambulance to the emergency room in the Westwood VA inpatient facility, more than fifteen miles away. Enough to send my panic attack out of stealth mode, had I actually been having a panic attack.

I wished I had something other than wondering what was wrong with my father to focus on, and felt guilty that I couldn't even be a good enough daughter to have a healthy panic attack. Something I had no control over was keeping me calm, cool, and collected. Possibly the fear of having an internal Humpty Dumpty crisis and finding that all the king's horses and all the king's men would not be able to put Dian back together again. I would have to take fear on as my friend for the time being.

Before the ambulance took my father away, he asked me for a favor. He wouldn't look me in the eye as he asked me to pick up his toiletry bag and some fresh underclothes. He hoped it wouldn't be a long stay, but his stays in Westwood were rarely short anymore. I didn't understand his discomfort in asking me until I arrived back at his house and opened his bedroom door.

My father rented a room from a friend of a friend. I hadn't actually met Max until that day. Max was a computer engineer who was nearly as untidy as my father. I walked past the living room full of computer monitors and keyboards and hard drives and motherboards and all the other components I could recognize but not name, and headed up the stairs to my father's bedroom. After living with my father for a short while as a teenager, I knew to expect an unkempt living space, but I could not have expected what I saw when I opened his bedroom door.

I was unable to see the floor. To the right was his bed, covered with debris: saw blades; a hammer; a box of nails; a plastic bag containing unopened cans of Campbell's Chunky soup; a seventeen-inch computer monitor I'd given him a year before; a box full of new and used and broken door knobs, hinges, and latches; nuts and bolts; a paper bag of fast food trash; empty Sprite cans; a cheeseburger wrapper; a few empty microwave dinner cartons and trays with most of the food eaten; business cards and stacks of paper; bills and file folders.

In all this mess on the bed, I wondered where he slept. On the opposite side of the mound there was a small space barely large enough for a small nine-year old boy, let alone a nearly six-foot-tall grown man. The pillow was dark with grease and dirt from his hair, which must have rarely been washed before he laid his head down on it. I pictured my father curled up in a fetal position just to fit into the space he'd left himself for sleeping, and tears streamed down my face.

There was no blanket, only a sheet that could be pulled halfway up to the top of the bed. It must have been months since the sheet had been changed. The other half of it was trapped under everything on the other side of the bed. *A person who lives like this just can't stay healthy.* I wondered if the chaos of my father's room had anything to do with him being perpetually ill. It certainly couldn't have helped.

My eyes searched the room for signs of the belongings my father had asked for. Aside from the bed, there were dirty and clean clothes, as well as sheets, blankets, duffle bags, books, videos, more bags of fast food trash and empty soda cups with dusty periscoped straws, and magazines strewn about the floor. This had to be months of my father walking into this room, undressing, and getting into bed after a long day's work without regard for having done the same thing night after night after night and not picking up a thing. I found unopened packages of both socks and underwear atop a stack of what looked to be clean clothes. I imagined he didn't have the energy to rummage through the mess to find undergarments, let alone to wash or fold them, so he just went out and bought new socks and underwear when he ran out of clean garments.

Caught up in the chaos, I could not avert my eyes from the rest of the room. To the left of the door, on the opposite side of the room from the bed, was his desk. It was filled with more stacks of paper, more file folders, more books and magazines and mail and letters and trash and bills, which all surrounded another computer monitor and covered the attached keyboard. A corkboard hung from the wall above the desk with a single piece of paper push-pinned to it. I recognized the handwriting immediately.

My own words, written to my father years ago. I stared at the letter, eyes blurred from tears, surrounded by the insurmountable mess. *What must my father think of himself to live like this?* I turned away from the corkboard, leaving the letter untouched. I stepped out of the bedroom and refused to think about what I'd written on that page.

I heard a creak on the stairs and turned around to see Max come around the corner. He was surprised to see me and saddened to learn that my father was back in the hospital. Max never asked for rent or money for bills my father was months behind on paying; he offered only his prayers for my father's wellness.

As Max retreated to his own room to leave me alone again, I began to feel trapped. I felt the need to flee, to get out of the mess and away from this realization of just how ill my father truly must be. I gathered up the toiletries he had asked for and decided he could never live here again. I drove back to the hospital and thought about how to have *that* conversation with my father.

Two months later, as I stood in front of my father in his ICU bed, there must have been a piece of me that realized we wouldn't have *any* further conversations. I might speak to him, he might nod or shake his head, but there would be no more father-daughter conversations with actual words.

Before the stroke and the hospice care and the last Christmas, my father had told me of how he and Pastor Ken and Carolyn would end their conversations. They'd say, "I'll see you on the other side." For them, it meant they'd see each other in heaven.

That in mind I said: "I'll do whatever it takes to see you on the other side."

I knew at the time what I was saying, and my father and Carolyn's version was not what I meant. I'm not even sure I knew what I meant at the time, but I wanted to put my father at ease. Tears continued to roll down his cheeks and fill his ears, spilling out and down his lobes. I continued to squeeze his hand, and while I knew that his "other side" and my "other side" were not the same place (although I do believe we might actually meet again some day), there was no need to explain that to him. I simply let him think whatever he thought, and left to go home for the night, leaving him in peace.

Day 4

Night poured rain into the morning. My windshield wipers slapped raindrop streams in the shape of a lopsided rainbow as I drove to the hospital. I wished my thoughts would wash away like the drops on the windshield, but like a dead bug, they stayed stuck.

I had absconded north and was away from my father when he needed me most. Maybe that was why he'd had the stroke to begin with. Maybe he missed me and couldn't bear to be without me, and he tried to die while I was away to keep from suffering anymore. Maybe he tried to die while I was away so I wouldn't have to be there for it. Or maybe neither one of us had anything to do with it, and it just happened the way it was supposed to.

During the night, the hospital staff had decided that my father's condition was no longer critical and had moved him out of the ICU into a room on the third floor. (The third floor was actually the fourth floor, but they don't talk about the basement being the morgue.)

I stepped into the nickel-plated elevator, a transporter of life and death lined with cold, surgical steel. I pressed the button for the third floor and waited. The polished, pristine metal emitted a sterile, tidy feeling. The elite-looking steel made me feel I was in a watered-down existence of reality. During the two floors up in my stainless compartment, nothing could be wrong. Everything was shiny and clean. Sterile. The buttons were all in order, the floors came one after the other, just like the digital numbers on the display said they would.

Stainless. Digital. Sterile.

I suppose these are all things one might want in a hospital. But it seemed somehow wrong to experience the realness of my father's process of dying in their perfect presence. That elevator, in all its magnificence, was the opposite of both life and death. It was the space between, where hope was possible in either.

While I waited for my floor to magically arrive in front of me when the doors spread open, I almost believed that I was there only to visit my ailing father. I almost believed that he would soon recover and I'd be able to take him back home with me. When the doors slid silently open in slow motion, I stepped into the hallway and looked for room 424.

Whatever hope I had gained on the elevator ride up evaporated into the icy, thin hospital air when I stepped into my father's room. The heart monitor steadily beat on my ears and on my nerves.

Just after my mother died my father took me to her townhouse at my grandmother's request. I was the only one who knew what things were hers and what things were her boyfriend's. My grandmother needed me to say, "Yes, this was Mom's; no this wasn't." My mother's boyfriend was in jail, and my grandparents wanted to make sure they got everything of my mother's before his brother, Henry, came to get his things. How would Henry know what was whose? He'd never been to the house in my eight years of knowing my mother's boyfriend.

I remember walking into the house. Coldness overtook me, and I trembled at the door. To the right at the entrance were the stairs to the second level. At the top of the stairs on the left, a door to my mother's bedroom. Beyond that bedroom, the hallway leading to my brother's bedroom—my old bedroom. A linen cabinet and shelves on the left, just before my bedroom door at the end of the hall. It had become David's room after I left. He had been in his room when four shots were fired in the room next door, two of which sent bullets into our mother's abdomen; he was just two and a half years old.

My grandmother wanted me to get things belonging to David and me from the bedroom. In order to get there I'd have to walk past my mother's bedroom. With closed eyes and a deep breath I almost forgot to release, I summoned every bit of strength at the bottom of the stairs.

I began to climb, one foot in front of the other, as I held the railing on the wall for support. As I ascended, the lower level became smaller and smaller, and the stairs became insurmountable. When I reached the halfway point, my legs gave out.

I slipped.

I fell just one step back and landed on my hands and knees, but I was too weak to continue. I sat on my knees and cried until my grandmother met me on the stairs to help me down and tell me it was okay. All I could say was, "I'm sorry."

I felt weak. Physically, emotionally, wholly. I felt like a failure. I had been asked to do one thing, and I had failed. I couldn't complete a simple task—to go up a single flight of stairs and pass a closed door to get to the belongings of my two-year-old brother. I feared they—my family and anyone else who would hear about my moment of failure—would always see me as Weak Little Dian, who couldn't even get halfway up the stairs without falling down on the job.

At times I still regret not going up there, as if I'd had a choice. I wonder if I'd breathed just a little bit deeper at the bottom of those stairs, would I have summoned enough strength to get to the top?

But I know the real issue didn't have anything to do with those stairs. I simply couldn't pass my mother's bedroom knowing even a few of the grisly details of what had gone on behind the now-closed door.

My father had warned me that the bedroom hadn't been cleaned up yet. The bedroom had been a crime scene. Wanting desperately to appear brave, I told him I could walk past the room if he closed the door. In the end, bravery had failed me, along with my weak legs. I didn't have to see anything in real life for my own imaginary version of what had happened in that room to play in my mind. I couldn't bring myself to be on the same level Steven or my mother had been on when those four shots were fired.

———∿∿⌒⊙⌒⊙⌒⊙⌒∿∿———

There were no shots fired during the last seven days of my father's life. But the constant beeping of the heart monitors was enough to drive me near mad. That and the awful green hospital gowns he spent those days in.

Upon entering my father's room after my pristine elevator ride, I saw he had a fresh set of linens and was wearing a clean but dingy green hospital gown.

Why do hospitals use such an awful, putrid, sickly green for patient gowns?

The faded pastel fabric brought out the yellowish jaundice in his skin, which made it look like rubbery chicken skin.

How nice.

His eyes seemed grayer than they'd been the day before, and the stubble on his cheeks and chin had grown into a three-day shadow. A sticky white residue from the tube in his throat being taped to his face for stability was left on his lips and stubble. The nurses and I wiped him down several times, but his face remained greasy from lack of a real bath or shower in more than four days. The flesh on his cheeks was rubbery and plastic. It felt as though it might stretch across the room just as it hung from his bones.

I had to work to recognize my father. My father, the man who always bailed me out. The man who always went to work. The man who honored his word as if it were the Bible's. The man who always believed in me. The man I could always count on to be there, wherever "there" was. He took me in when my mother turned me out. He found a parent and youth support group and taught me how to communicate. He knew the good, the bad, and the ugly about me, and he loved me anyway. He had done the unflattering due diligence only a father with faith would do, and I felt as if I had only marginally repaid him. As I stared at this man who had been a part of my last thirty years, I wondered who would be there to love me unconditionally when he was gone.

Wrapped up in this question, I ceased to remember any day that did not fit a fantasy. Gone were the fights over bedtime and whether or not I would go to work with him the following day. Gone were the arguments over religion and politics and sexuality. Gone were the judgments either of us housed against the other for any and all of those things. The only memories that remained were the Friday nights of softball; the Saturday mornings I sat in his truck amusing myself while he worked before I got bored enough to find out what he actually did all day long; the Sunday mornings of my childhood when his men's softball league would bet dollars on the outcome of the game and lay the bills in the rain to pay the other team when they lost; in adulthood, my Monday night softball games he attended religiously, he in the stands and me stepping to the plate as if I were someone special; and the Sunday afternoons he spent after church on my couch where we talked about everything and nothing at all.

Through memory's tunnel vision, I saw the softball games he took me to, the plays he made in the field, the doubles he hit, the slides he slid, the RBIs he knocked in, the walks he took for the sake of the team. I saw every softball game I ever watched him play.

He had an air of confidence when he stepped onto a softball field. He visualized himself diving for the ball and making the catch. He knew—in a way that one knows that the sun will rise every morning—that when he stood at the plate he was going to hit the ball hard and hit it far. He knew that, when he let go of the ball from the outfield, it would end up in the infielder's glove he'd intended it for. He'd been playing baseball since he was five years old, and softball was just a slower version that gave him plenty of time to perfect his swing while he stood in the batter's box. He was good because he loved every second of it.

I found myself wishing he'd lived the rest of his life like that.

My father had been reintubated after the room change, which left his throat and mouth bloody because of his resistance to the process. The nurse gave me some long, cotton-tipped swabs dipped in sterilizing foam to clean his mouth. Using the medicated swab, I scraped as much dried blood as I could from his tongue, teeth, and the walls of his mouth, but couldn't get it all.

My stomach churned, dropped, rose, then sank again as chunks of dried blood came off his teeth and the roof of his mouth while I swabbed. I nearly lost whatever food I'd eaten that morning, but continued to clean. My father attempted to move his left arm while his right arm lay limp from the stroke, and IVs and tubes and wires that attached his body to machines kept him tied to the bed. He had been a Jerry-of-all-trades for nearly thirty years, and now he couldn't lift his hand to clean the inside of his mouth. His eyes were sunken; the skin on his face lay like cactus, dry and unkempt. His eyes took on a sadness that I recognized from Christmas: *One more thing I can't do for myself.*

AJ, a friend of the family, visited my father nearly every day. I'd always known her as AJ and had never asked what the initials stood for. One morning after my father had fallen asleep, I caught her looking at me as if she wanted to say something but didn't know how.

"You know I took care of your Nana Helen when she had breast cancer," she said. "She was in so much pain at the end there, and it was the best thing we could have done for her, to start that morphine."

She looked at my father and said, "Oh, how he loved your Nana Helen." She gave him a kiss on the cheek, hugged me, and left.

My father and I had never had a conversation specifically about morphine. But we did have conversations about how he wanted to live, and under which circumstances he did not.

His words: "I don't want to be a vegetable, Dian."

He didn't want me or anyone else to suffer. At the end, he just wanted peace for himself and for those he loved. But how was I supposed to find peace while sitting in that hospital room watching him die in pain? How could I just ignore his words?

During my rebellious teenage years, my father was a part of the parent/youth support group, Because I Love You. As a part of a series of weekend workshops, over a period of fifteen years, we had a chance to write more than ten letters to each other as if we were never going to see each other again. He had pinned one of the letters I'd written to him onto the corkboard above his desk. It began with these words: "I love you. You are the most wonderful, loving, and giving man I've ever met, and I'm so very proud to call you my father."

Maybe, at the end, we all just want that letter.

I sat alone with him in silence until just after ten in the evening. Outside in the parking lot, sheets of rain were still falling, keeping Reese up north for one more night. I cursed the weather, wanting nothing more than to cast my sore eyes on her soft, perfect, loving face. I wanted to feel wisps of her nut-brown hair tickle my ears as she held my body close to hers. I wanted to feel the warmth of her body, her arms, her skin, her lips pressed up against mine. I wanted to kiss her and for her to kiss me. I wasn't thinking about sex, but an intimate, human moment in which I could hold on to my girlfriend and simply be loved. I told her I'd rather she wait another day and be safe than drive on a slippery, stormy road through the armpit of California just because I missed her, but that was a lie. What I really wanted was for her to risk life and limb to get to me, to be with me, to hold me as I wanted to hold her. I wanted to hear ballads booming in the background as I pictured her driving through rain and sleet, singing about ain't no mountain high enough. Instead, I kept my ballads to myself while she stayed safe and I stayed alone for one more night.

Day 5

The next morning, heavy rain escorted me to the hospital. I walked from my car, through the rain, sans umbrella, into the hospital lobby.

My father had been transferred to yet another room. Overnight, he had started having seizures, the nurse told me. I'd never seen anyone actually have a seizure before. When I was in high school, I saw a boy have what I thought was a seizure, but I learned later that he had faked it for attention.

Some significant differences between my father's seizure and the faked one: my father's eyes rolled back into his head. His cheek muscles contorted in a way I'd never seen before—or have seen duplicated since. He was visibly fatigued when the seizure was over, and didn't recall anything.

The high school faker had none of those things, only some heavy breathing and animated flopping about on the floor while a classroom full of juniors stared on in silence.

According to the doctors, there was no obvious reason for the seizures. They thought he may have had more strokes, but couldn't be sure without running intrusive tests.

My father's older brother Johnny and his wife, Bertha, brought their kids to visit. John Jr. was eight; Selena was twelve. My father spent most of the day asleep, and was awake only for short intervals of a halfway silent conversation and the intermittent seizures. He didn't appear to be in very much pain—at least, he didn't complain about whatever pain he felt—and seemed to be aware of his surroundings when he was awake. My father's visitors went in and out of keeping him involved in the conversation, and when he dozed off, the conversation shifted from engaging my father to talking about his condition.

At one point, we stood in a circle beside my father's bed while he slept. We talked in low voices about the funeral, the burial, the death, and all their intertwining parts and pieces. During the conversation, someone noticed a pair of small, shiny black shoes sticking out from the bottom of the bed curtain. Selena had pulled back toward the wall and wrapped the curtain around herself, silent tears streaming down her cheeks. Johnny stepped into the curtain with her to find out what she was doing.

She said she'd held her hands over her ears because she hadn't wanted to hear the conversation of her Uncle Jerry's death. When that didn't work, she'd stood behind the curtain, wrapped it around herself, and prayed. I wished any of that would help.

Johnny took Selena into the hallway to talk to her and help her calm down. When she came back into the room she stood tall next to my father and looked back toward her own. On Johnny's cue, we stepped away to give her some privacy. She took her uncle's hand and said a prayer. I heard only the end: "I pray that you get better soon, Jerry."

I hope that works, kid.

Johnny stepped outside with Bertha and the kids while Rick and I continued the talk of where my father would be buried. Nana Helen, my father's mother, was buried at Forest Lawn in the Hollywood Hills, and while my father wanted to be buried near her, he couldn't afford a plot on the property, let alone one near her. I mentioned that he told me that he would be happy with the VA burial because it was free and wouldn't place a financial burden on any of us. I also mentioned that I didn't give a shit about the cost, and I wanted him to be buried wherever he wanted to be buried, even if that meant I had to pay for it myself. That wouldn't be necessary, as we all agreed to split the cost of a plot at Forest Lawn, and that was that.

It's not that I wanted to talk about my father getting buried. I just couldn't bear not to; I knew time would not permit. I stood at my father's bedside and listened to us all make decisions about his funeral, and wondered if I could survive another death.

March 2003.

A phone call. Sunday night: Grandpa had just left for Europe and Grandma couldn't be happier to have the house to herself, along with some peace and quiet. Grandma and Grandpa's relationship was such that, until I was about thirteen, I thought Grandma had never left Grandpa because divorce wasn't legal back in "those days." I later learned that divorce had been legal all her life, but that she had made a conscious choice to stay because she'd learned how to deal with my grandfather. That, and she hadn't worked since January 1953 and had made up her mind that she never would again. She always said, "He can be a mean SOB, but I don't have to deal with him when he goes on his trips." And Grandpa was always going on a trip. By the time I was twenty-five, Grandpa was on a trip to Europe or Hawaii or San Diego or Florida for four days or three weeks or two months for nearly six months out of the year. When Grandma got sick of him, she'd suggest he go on a trip, and he'd gladly oblige.

The night my grandfather left for his nine-week trip across Europe, their neighbors brought my grandmother some home-cooked Armenian food. She presumed their visit was more to check in on her than to bring her the food, but she wasn't feeling well and didn't much care for the food or the company that night, as she told me over the phone when she called to tell me about Grandpa's departure. She had a headache and would take half of a Fiorinal—a full one would knock her silly, she said—and feel better in the morning. Grandma's phone calls with me were often less about the information exchanged and more about the simple connection of grandmother and granddaughter.

Monday morning: the beginning of a busy day. Phone calls and back orders and wrong shipments and defective parts and broken light bulbs and e-mail after e-mail after e-mail; the day never seemed to end, yet I hadn't even had lunch yet. By the time I thought about eating, it was two o'clock and one of my employees sent me to lunch—that is to say, she refused to work with me for the remaining two hours of her workday unless I ate something. Food in my stomach was best for us all.

Lunch time: As I walked to my car I decided to pick up El Pollo Loco for lunch—something for myself and a Pollo Bowl for Grandma—take it to her house, and eat with her. On the way to El Pollo Loco I made a right turn instead of a left, which led me to Grandma's house instead of to the chicken joint. I decided to get her out of the house and take her to the bowl, rather than take the food to her.

Grandma's house: I entered the side door (we understand the front door to be for sales people and unknown visitors who didn't frequent the house enough to know that we used the side door like the front door). Once I entered the house, I heard the sound of a TV. *Grandma must have her hearing aids out.* I shouted, "Grandma! Hellooooo . . ." She didn't like to be surprised. Said I almost gave her a heart attack one time when I came in, even though I was sure I'd been loud enough not to scare her. I went through the kitchen, left into the hallway, past Grandpa's stamp room, past the door on the left to the front of the house and the formal dining room, toward the sound of the TV in the bedroom at the end of the hallway. One last shout before I reach the master bedroom and turn the corner: "Grandmoooo . . . hellooooooo!"

A half step into the bedroom. TV blaring by her side of the bed. Bed unmade and empty. In the split second it took me to turn to my right at the door and take another step into the room and toward the door of the attached bathroom, I thought: *She must have just gotten out of the shower.* My foot fell into my second step and I suddenly had a clear view of the bathroom.

My heart. Sank. I thought I heard it fall to the floor and smash into a million pieces next to my grandmother. She was face down, and blood and saliva were spilling from her mouth, probably from the fall, but I wouldn't think about that until later. I rushed to her and bent down to help her up. I touched her back. I recognized the coldness of her skin. A flash to my mother's casket: my hand on hers, when I first felt the coldness that can come only from death. Back in the bathroom, my mind raced. *What do I do? What do I do? What do I do!* I always thought I'd know exactly what to do in an emergency, but then, the moment had ceased to be an emergency by the time I arrived.

I found the phone in the bedroom on the table next to the sliding glass window. I picked it up. I dialed numbers. I paced into the hallway and into the formal dining room. I saw myself in the mirror-tiled wall. I saw fragmented pieces of my sunken soul. I turned away from myself as a man answered the other end of the line. "Hi, Bob," I said, "it's Dian . . ." I paused, unable to speak. "What is it?" he asked. "Grandma," I said, my voice cracking. And I was unable to say another word. Bob understood what I couldn't speak about his mother. "Oh, God, you're not telling me . . ." I heard a thud on the other end of the line. He'd fallen to his knees, and I still had no words for him. He asked what had happened. I said I came for lunch and found her. "Did you call the paramedics?" he asked me. "No. I didn't know what to do . . . I called *you*." A few more words back and forth. I hung up to call 911.

A female operator answered the line: "911, what's your emergency?" *If I know she's dead is this really an emergency?* I told her my "situation." She asked if my grandmother was breathing. I said, "I don't think so. She's so cold." The operator asked me if I could turn my grandmother over so she could walk me through performing CPR. I was horrified at the thought. I balked. I knew she was dead. I *knew* the cold feeling. The operator pushed. I began to cry. I was in disbelief.

Is this really happening? How can I do this? I went back into the bathroom, cordless phone in hand. I stooped down next to my grandmother and set the phone down. I tried to turn her over, but just as strength had failed me on the stairs in my mother's townhouse twelve years before, I could not bring myself to turn my grandmother over. I picked up the cordless phone and told the operator, "I'm sorry. I'm so sorry." And I sobbed. She told me it was okay and that the paramedics were on their way. She would stay with me on the line until they arrived.

Sirens in the background. I'd heard them many times before as they found their way to the nursing home just a mile down the road. But this time the sirens were closer, and getting closer still. An ambulance found its way to the driveway. A fire truck followed close behind. I hung up the phone and showed the men into the house, into the bedroom, and into the master bathroom. I left them to their business and sat in the breakfast nook off the kitchen in a painted white wicker chair and rocked back and forth until one of them appeared in the doorway. "I'm sorry for your loss," he said. "She expired some time ago."

A quiet calm—numbness, no doubt—came over me. There was nothing more I could do.

I sat in my red polo shirt and black slacks and wondered how I would survive another death.

Johnny and his oldest son, Isaac, found a plot at Forest Lawn on a grassy hill that overlooked the San Fernando Valley. They wanted Rick and me to meet them there to check out the plot and agree on the spot my father would be buried. I opted not to go; if they approved, I had no reason not to.

Rick, Johnny, and Isaac walked into Forest Lawn's mortuary and funeral services office to finalize the purchase of my father's plot. Johnny and Isaac had been there before and met with a tiny European man with an accent who had shown them the grassy knoll where my father would be buried. The same man greeted them when they walked in the door. Rick expected a hello or a courtesy smile and head tilt silently asking, "How are you?" but not really meaning it. He received neither. Instead, the accented European man said to the three of them, "Dead yet?" My family has always had a dry sense of humor, so they were hardly fazed while in the European man's presence.

Upon exiting the funeral home, they could hold back their laughter no more. Isaac mimicked the European man's accent and carried on his part in any conversation on the way back to the hospital in that accent. My uncles and cousin laughed their low laughs and, while in awe of the man's audacity and directness, found a way to also appreciate the humor. I guess we all needed to feel something "normal."

And besides, no, he wasn't dead yet.

When they returned from Forest Lawn after securing the plot, Rick, Johnny, and I told my father about it. They described the near-empty-of-plots hill he'd be stationed on. They described the short walk uphill they would take to visit their mother. They described the view of the valley from my father's future plot. He was unable to speak as silent tears rolled down his cheeks. I became aware that I had no idea why he was crying.

Maybe it was happiness about being buried in the same resting place as his mother. My father had done genealogy research during the year before his death and discovered that there were several members of our family tree buried at that site. He felt a pull to be a part of *that* history in *that* cemetery—as though his final resting place ought to be there, with his family.

Maybe he wished he could thank us for being there for him, not just then, but all his life. Maybe he was sad he couldn't use his words. I imagined my father flashing back to childhood, to brotherhood, with these now-grown men in front of him, and then back to my own birth and everything that my life somehow gave him.

Maybe it was a combination of all of these things. Or maybe it was something I didn't have the sense to imagine.

Things between Reese and me began to fall apart in February 2005. We went to dinner with Dave, a close friend and mentor of mine, and Dave asked Reese questions that made me cringe. Questions about the future and her path to get there, questions about her life's wants and needs and desires and what she intended to do about making them reality. In all honesty, it wasn't the questions that made me cringe; it was her answers. I sat beside her, listening to Dave ask her questions I'd always wanted to know the answers to but never had the courage to ask. She and I were just supposed to have some summer fun—a summer fun fling (even though one of us hoped, dreamed, and silently speculated for more). He wasn't supposed to ask the deep questions about what the future held. Reese answered Dave's questions simply and openly. She answered the questions in detail and with poised thought. And she answered the questions as if we were not a couple. As if she were answering them only for herself. As if he were not asking her the questions to lead her to say something that would land the two of us together forever. Or maybe she just answered the questions honestly.

Maybe our paths were not destined to unfold side by side until eternity. I couldn't bear the thought of being alone. I felt my skin sink deep inside my body, my insides raw and exposed. I couldn't fathom it on a conscious level, but the answers Reese gave to Dave's questions revealed fundamental differences between us that could not be salvaged by love or affection for one another. On a conscious level, I knew I needed to know the answers to those questions, regardless of the knots they created in my stomach. I allowed my mentor to carry my courage through his questions, though I knew I would be unwilling to change course until . . . well, until after my father was gone.

I couldn't fathom a time I'd willingly part with Reese, but I decided it would never come at my hands. Having some sense of how our relationship might be affected, I almost hated Dave for inciting truth's bright light that night. The knots in my stomach spelled out clearly for me, "This is the beginning of the end."

Dave didn't have the fear of Reese leaving me that I had; he had no reason not to ask his questions. *Where do you see yourself in five years? How do you feel about living in Los Angeles? Family? Kids? How do these all tie together for you?*

Of course, Dave asked the same questions of me, and I came up with some bullshit answers, attempting to mirror what I thought Reese might say or create something she'd want to hear. "I wouldn't mind living outside of LA," rather than, "I love LA! It's my home and can't imagine leaving anytime soon." Or an even more truthful version: "I love LA! It's my home and I don't want to leave, but I'd do anything this woman asked me to, even if I knew I'd be miserable in some other state, far away from my father." Then, "At some point I think I want kids," came out, instead of the truth: "I've wanted kids my whole life and can't wait to be a mom." I'd thought about having kids with Reese, sure, but right at that point I had to pretend that it was fine that we didn't even talk about living together.

In reality, no one was moving anywhere or starting a family. Not Reese, not me, and certainly not us together. But in my head I had created a land where love conquered all, and she couldn't wait to cohabit with me and have two kids with me and stay in LA with me and raise a family with me and live happily ever after with me. I had expectations of Reese she never even knew about, and I wasn't about to share them with her there, with my mentor free to ask his questions and rip truth or the end of our relationship right out of me.

Of course, my relationship with Reese wasn't the only one I held silent expectations in.

As for sensing the end was near in February, I had been right, no matter how much I didn't want to be. Just a year later, things would be so different I would hardly recognize either of us.

But before the end there was that day in July of 2005 when I fell completely apart. It was, sadly, just the middle of the end. I thought it was about everything outside of my relationship, but looking back now with hindsight's clear vision, I realize it was about the way I handled *everything* in my life: Deal only with what you have to, leave the rest for later. And pretend "later" will never come.

I had breakfast with Reese at a restaurant on a Saturday morning after dropping her car off at a dealership in Pasadena for an oil change. Bad breakfast. (Was it the breakfast that was bad or this *thing* brewing inside me?) I had driven around for thirty minutes trying to find a restaurant that was even open. I had driven around after our bad breakfast to find a quiet place where we could leisurely wait for her car to be ready. I turned slowly around a corner to a side street, contemplating whether or not the park on the right was a good place to sit and wait. An impatient man in the SUV behind me honked violently and sped around us. I sped up trying to not let him pass and screamed out the window: *"Fuuuuuuuck yoooooooouuuuu!"*

Reese stared at me with an eerie look on her face. Calmly, quietly she said, "Baby, pull over." I did. I put the gearshift in park, and without killing the engine, I put my head in my hands and began to sob. Uncontrollable tears streamed down my face. For the first time since my grandmother died, I allowed myself to cry like this. For the first time in almost ten years I allowed myself to be this way in plain view of a civilian. Any crying I'd done had been like a military operation, as far back as I can remember. This time, I sat and sobbed for what seemed like an eternity, sharing more of myself with Reese in those wordless moments than I had in over a year of being in a relationship with her.

She sat with me as I sobbed, touching my leg, my hand, holding me when I moved close enough—as close as bucket seats would allow—unsure of what more she could do, of what more I needed. She waited. I imagine she was waiting for a sign of how to help the agony wash away, both hers and mine. I imagine she was waiting to learn more about a woman she was in love with but didn't completely know or understand. I had shut her out—knowingly, unknowingly—afraid of what might run through her head if she knew the fears keeping pace with my silence.

So much guilt in me. So much shame for not being strong enough to handle everything on my own. My grandfather had been sick for months, but had only recently let on how bad it had gotten. If it had been up to him, he would have followed suit with many men who died within six months of their wives' passing. But nearly a decade before my grandmother's death, he'd had a massive heart attack. Doctors had placed a defibrillator just under the skin of his chest to kick start his heart should it attempt to give out on him again. At the time of his surgery, he'd been ecstatic to get approved for such a measure, being in his mid seventies. With his wife now dead for nearly two years, I wonder if he wished he'd never had the surgery in the first place. Defibrillator or not, his heart and the rest of his body had begun the process of letting go of my grandfather's life on earth. He was unstable on his feet but insisted on walking the quarter mile to the grocery store every week rather than get a ride or drive. Immediately following my grandmother's death, I moved in with my grandfather to help him through the initial shock of having the three-bedroom house all to himself, but I'd since moved back out on my own once he was settled. My office was still a mile from the house, though, and I would check in on him nearly every day. I'd enter the house to see him fully reclined in his La-Z-Boy, facing the television, mouth agape, looking as if he was barely breathing, if at all. Sometimes I'd walk back out, slam the door, and quickly open it just so he'd wake and hear me come in.

As I sobbed in the car on a warm Pasadena morning, my mind raced around an Indy track of fears and what-ifs and how-can-Is as I thought about my grandfather's condition.

How can I be expected to go into his house every day? Go in there every day and not fear finding him dead on the bathroom floor? One person can only take so much. He's so old and frail. His mind works most of the time, but his body just can't keep up.

I fear that I'll have to watch it all unfold and be a part of it. I fear that he'll die in his home and I'll bear witness to the aftermath of yet another death that touches my already-too-scarred-to-heal wound. I fear I'll go there every day and hold my breath walking down the hall when he can't hear my calls because his ESPN is turned up so loud I can hear it from the driveway. When he doesn't respond, I have flashes of my grandmother dead on the floor, blood spilling out of the corner of her mouth from the fall. I can't remember that every day. It's too much for me.

Sobbing in Reese's arms, I couldn't know yet that my grandfather would last only another two months. He would die just two days after being admitted to hospice care. Knowing that might've helped me pull myself together some. Instead, what helped were old habits: Deal only with what you have to, Dian. Keep your silent expectations to yourself.

Another seizure struck. The seizures were relatively short and mild according to the nurses, but seeing my father tense up with his eyes sputtered back in his head, unable to control his awkward and jerky convulsions made me fear otherwise. I had counted ten seizures to that point, and asked the nurse if I should be concerned about the number, or even the fact that he was having them at all. She sympathetically told me that he didn't remember much of them, if anything at all. She then said that the seizures probably weren't helping his condition, and asked if anyone was available to stay the night with him.

There was a brief moment of pause as people in the room took deep breaths and tried to scour their minds for plans and excuses for why they couldn't stay. At least, that's what I did. But before I finished my thought, I heard myself say that I would stay. I wondered if I'd volunteered to stay for love or martyrdom. Either way, I knew my father would do the same for me, so I listened as the nurse gave instructions for taking care of him, should he have a seizure while there were just the two of us in the room.

She told me it was important he lay on his side when a seizure occurred so he didn't choke on his tongue. Important that I turn him—his face, his body—on his side when he began to seize.

"I realize his condition," she said, "but you don't want him to go *that way*."

I took a piece of paper from a drawer in the room. I drew three columns. Time. Duration. Magnitude. I felt like a reporter. I didn't feel as if I was my father's daughter at all.

My father's eyes stared off as if he saw something beyond me. I looked behind me and there was nothing there. I looked back at him. He was not convulsing. His hands and arms were pulled up close into his body as if he was trying to keep warm. He began to shake. The mild ones lasted ten to thirty seconds. The moderate ones lasted thirty to ninety seconds. The shaking grew increasingly stronger until the last few seconds. The violent seizures made it difficult to hold him on his side. The shaking shifted to jolting. There were two of the violent seizures. The first one lasted fifty-eight seconds. The second one lasted one minute, twelve seconds.

I can't believe I'm here.

I tried to read. I picked up an outdated *People* magazine and thumbed to find the cover article, "Jen Breaks her Silence." I found the article. Four sentences in, my father's seizure reclaimed my attention.

I tried to watch TV. The hospital room television seemed to have more cable channels than I did at home, and I flipped and flipped and flipped hoping something would catch my attention. What caught my attention instead was another seizure.

Magazine closed, television off, my mind drifted to Reese. A simple thought, *I hope she's sleeping well.* I thought about Sly and Killer and had no doubts my cats were sleeping well. I thought about my father visiting me on Sundays. He always dressed well for God, and I enjoyed seeing him after church in a button-up shirt and dress slacks, complete with fancy tie, shiny belt, and shoes.

Another seizure.

An image of Sly, as he hissed at my father. His black-and-white fur stood up on his back as he edged closer to my father. When he recognized my father's scent, he jumped onto his lap. My father stroked Sly's ears and back and belly. A heap of black-and-white fur was left on my father's Sunday church suit. My father smiled and stroked Sly's fur some more.

Another seizure.

I looked at the time and noted the minute hand and the second hand. I reached over the bed railing and pushed my father's left side above his right side. His jaw did not bite down on his tongue.

When I was fourteen I was arrested for shoplifting from a Mervyn's department store, and my father picked me up at the police station. There was no reason to believe I was a flight risk, and they let my father take me. He was house sitting for his best friend from junior high school, Roy, and that's where my father took me that night. The house wasn't far from his apartment, but he figured it was far enough that I wouldn't try to sneak out to see my friends. Within an hour of arriving, I crawled through Roy's second-floor bathroom window and jumped onto the roof of the garage. From the roof, I jumped onto the driveway and walked down the street, determined to create a different life and never look back.

Six weeks later, I found myself lonely, homesick, and afraid I was never going to amount to anything. I arranged a meeting with Because I Love You, and they arranged a meeting with my parents on the next day. My father was the only one who met me—my mother didn't believe I would show up. My father prayed I would. He told me he always believed that I was worth even the slightest possibility.

That's how I felt about my father on the night of all the seizures: he was worth even the slightest possibility of life. And I didn't want him to go *that* way.

Day 6

Tests run on the morning of the sixth day of my father's hospital stay suggested he had suffered several small strokes during the previous day and night. The neurologist told us it was possible they had been triggered by the seizures, or maybe vice versa.

They could operate, but there was no guarantee my father would survive. And what if he did? Would his quality of life be any better? Would he talk again? Walk again?

Rick, Johnny, and I agreed that surgery wouldn't fix anything. There would be no operation. *So, what next?* I asked Rick and Johnny what they thought about giving my father morphine to ease his pain. They supported me in whatever decision I chose to make and turned the question back to me.

Visions of the DNR forms flashed in my mind. "I don't want to be a vegetable, Dian."

The day I started morphine would be the last day I'd be able to tell my father anything he'd hear or understand or respond to. No more hand squeezes or head nods. No more eye contact. No more communication of any kind between the two of us.

A flashback to just three days before Christmas (was it only a week ago now?): A conversation between father and daughter.

I sat on the couch next to my father. Somewhere in what turned out to be the middle of the conversation I asked him why he never asked me about Reese.

The look on his face stays with me, still. Reserved. Taken aback. Shocked. Thoughtful. Reverential. And then, "I don't know." A pause. A long pause.

My father had a way of pausing that left you wondering just how long he was going to think before he answered. And sometimes he wouldn't. Sometimes I would wait and wait and wait and no answer would come. He would get so lost in thought that he was no longer thinking about an answer to a question, but had long since moved away, further, deeper into his brain for answers from a different time.

He might have gone from Reese to Carla; from Carla to debates; from debates to high school; high school to car clubs; car clubs to the '57 Mustang he wanted to buy in the eleventh grade but his step-father wouldn't let him on account of living less than a mile from the high school; '57 Mustang to what a bastard Charles was for that deprivation. And then all at once he'd look up and find me staring at him, waiting for an answer to a question he'd long since forgotten. My father knew there was a question, but now it seemed to have escaped his mind, hiding amongst the debates and the clubs and the bastard. So, he sat in silence and even looked away. No smile, no acknowledgement, just a sly twitch of the eye and a hollow twist of the cheek to mask what I had written off as his embarrassment.

And then, as if from nowhere: "I guess I'm just afraid I'll like her." An answer that seemed to seep from behind the curtains of my father's brain. Could it be he wasn't embarrassed? Could it be that he truly was giving the question its due thought? Could it be that all these years I just didn't give him time enough to answer me?

He had liked Carla. He'd come over every Sunday after church and sit with me and watch baseball and talk about sports, news, the economy, his business, my promotion, the tire he had to replace on his truck (again), the test for his contractor's license, my new car, Grandma's health, Grandpa's latest trip to Germany or San Diego or Florida, the weather, or any other topic we could chew on in avoidance of politics or religion or (*shhhh!*) my sexuality. When he arrived before I was quite ready, he'd sit in the living room and talk to Carla. Their conversations were different than the ones I had with him. They'd talk about religion and politics and get into debates on who did what right and which morals were in place, and the ethics that were or weren't being questioned by so and so, or whether or not the president ought to have done this or that. At the end of those conversations, they were all smiles, sitting in sheer enjoyment of exercising their minds and expanding viewpoints, regardless of whose they were.

For me, it wasn't that easy. Emotion tended to get the best of me during debates with my father, which made it more of an exercise for my heart than my mind. I often wished I'd grown up spending more time with my father, just to learn how to debate without letting my emotions unravel me. But we grow up how we grow up, and I assumed nothing would change the way my father and I conversed, especially when it came to our mutually silent decision to not talk about the things we disagreed upon.

My father and Carla especially enjoyed those types of conversations. She and my father reveled in the process of breaking down both topics and people for the sake of discussion, then building them back up just the way they saw them. Carla was enamored of my father's quiet passion for anything he believed in, and she always wanted to know more—more about what he thought about God and how He had found His way into my father's life. More about President Bush and just what good my father believed he was doing for the country. More about the Reagan Administration and everything my father had come to realize it had done right. More about the Vietnam War and how it had changed America, and especially how it had changed my father. Carla was always thirsty for a different perspective, just so she could see another side, because there always was another side, and my father appreciated this. Their quiet manners of resonance, dissonance, and passion both complimented and inspired one another. I could only sit and marvel (or completely tune out), remaining happily unengaged.

When Carla and I broke up, my father was both heartbroken and hopeful. Heartbroken that I had to hurt, even if I was the one who'd initiated it. He liked Carla and would miss their conversations, but I saw his sadness having more to do with watching his daughter slowly walk herself through heartache. The hopefulness was the selfish side of him that wanted to see me live a life of "good Christian values." *His* Christian values. He was certain that if things didn't work out between Carla and me that I would give dating men another chance. I'd even said as much in the process of bringing my relationship with Carla to an end.

Just as some women swear off men and toy with the idea of finding a nice girl to settle down with for the rest of their lives, I breathed about swearing off women. It wasn't that I really wanted to be with a man; it was that I didn't want my heart broken again. A surefire way for a lesbian to never have a broken heart is to spend the rest of her life with a man. Of course, that's also a surefire way to never be happy again.

In the beginning of our relationship, I believed that Carla was The One—yes, women tend to do this in the beginning, gay or straight. As our relationship wore on, I thought, *If things don't work out between us, maybe I'll just find a man and* make *it work.* And just as the woman who swears off men after her heartbreak does, I came to my senses when I was no longer emotional and delirious, memory's bright eye recalling, *So yeah, umm . . . you're not straight, Dian; remember, we've already been through this.* And once again, my father was heartbroken.

When I began to date Reese, he didn't want to relive that heartache. He preferred to ask about me and my Dodgers and my apartment and my cats and my softball and my job and my raise and my new car and my anything-and-anyone-other-than-Reese. And I accepted that. Until I couldn't, three days before Christmas in 2005.

We knew his death was imminent, looming around the corner; we could smell it if we put our noses to the ground like hounds or in the air like retrievers.

I needed to know why he avoided the topic of my girlfriend. I needed to know why he refused to refer to her as my girlfriend and would only call her my "friend," and with that change in intonation, as if he knew there was more to it but wasn't willing to acknowledge it. I needed to express my anger and frustration with the idea that he didn't accept me for who I was and the way I lived my life. I needed to know why he didn't accept me. His daughter. His blood. The only blood he's ever had a hand in creating. And all at once, it became clear: he didn't understand me; he didn't even *know* me. *I must* make *him understand.*

As I launched into a speech about how he didn't know me and didn't accept me and didn't honor my beliefs because they were different from his, my heart raced and I realized that I'd authorized this behavior from the beginning. I didn't invite him to discuss our beliefs because it was uncomfortable. Not for him, but for me. I'd been pointing the finger at my father all this time and I'd been neglecting the truth about myself all the while: I never *allowed* my father to accept me because I never revealed the whole of who I really was . . . who I'd come to be. And yet, I couldn't bring these thoughts out from the shadows and into the light of conversation. I didn't know how. So I just kept talking about God only knows what.

I began to hear myself speak as if I were a teacher on the *Peanuts* cartoon: *waah wahh, wahh waahwah.* My father waited for me to pause before he quietly said, "Dian, you're right. I don't even know what you believe."

And then: "I want to know what you believe."

Dumbfounded from his admission and still feigning for control of the situation, I retorted with, "Okay, but you have to listen. This isn't a debate. This isn't an opportunity for you to step in and tell me where I'm wrong; this is where I get to tell you what I believe. And you just get to listen."

He agreed.

I went on to justify my demand, although my father clearly didn't require it: "I just want to get it all out and not get distracted and not get caught off guard. I just want to share this with you." A pause. "And then maybe we can talk about it."

"Okay."

I told him about my belief in God and of the Universe and connection to source and souls. Of my belief that I'd been here before, that I was an "old soul" and this will not be my last time here. Of my belief in a power greater than myself, though it's nothing like an old man with a white beard who presides over all the land and sends his son to the earth to teach us. Of the idea that we are all part of God, or the Universe, or whatever it is that created us all. Of the idea that there is more here than we know what to do with; that we were all created in love and with love and for love, and if we all exercised just that part of ourselves, we would all be living well. Of a world where people are not wrong for sharing love with another human being. Of a world where Jesus was a great man with many great things to teach; where we are all sons and daughters of God, and we do not judge each other because we interpret God, the Universe, and their intentions differently.

I told him of my belief that there is no heaven, no hell, no afterlife where all is bliss for some and the rest are damned for all of eternity. Of my belief that love and the human capacity to both give and receive it unconditionally (whether we choose to honor that capacity or not) is what makes this world go around. Of an idea that God, the Universe, a higher power is not here to judge me or have others judge me, but to love me and show me more ways to love and find love to give and share, and that all of this is somehow related to my purpose for being here at all.

My father was silent. Shaken. Sunken.

"I—I had no idea," he stammered. "I'm dumbfounded. I had no idea that this was your belief in God. I—I thought I had twenty years left to show you the greatness of Jesus and now—now, I don't know. And you're so far from what . . . so far . . . it's so different. I'm not sure you'll ever see The Way . . ." he trailed off and stared blankly at me trying to figure out what came next.

My voice trembled and I felt a shiver crawl from my bones to my skin. *What if I keep talking and he decides to not love me anymore?* I spoke through the shivers: "Yeah, what I believe is far away from what you believe; you believe I'm going to hell for loving another woman, and I believe I'm living my life the best way I know how." I searched for the words that best expressed my heart and kept talking. "This isn't something I chose for myself; it's just the way it is. I can no more marry a man in good conscience than you could. My life may not be what *you* want it to be, but it's a life I'm proud of. I'm not proud of everything I've ever done, but I've learned from it all, and I'm a good person. And I'm certainly not going to hell for loving another woman."

Quietly and almost to no one, he said, "I'm not even sure that's what I believe anymore."

Just a week ago, all those questions unasked and statements unstated had been put out in the open air so they could live and breathe and not die with the man sitting in the sunken couch with cushions that ought to have been replaced years ago. A decision about morphine would not change that.

Rick and Johnny looked at me, waiting for a decision.

"Start the morphine drip."

Rick and Johnny nodded, I sensed in relief.

When visitors left my father's hospital room, I was envious of them. I thought of them as going back to life.

Back to life. Ha.

I couldn't think about getting back to any kind of life until my father was gone. I just wanted it all to be over and to go back to something that wasn't *this*. Something normal. I had to get back to normal.

But there was no such thing as normal anymore. The normal I had once known had died. I had gone from knowing for sure that my father would show up to my softball games to wondering when I'd see him again. I had gone from him being in my weekly thoughts to worrying on a daily basis how he was responding to the chemo and radiation treatments. I had gone from working sixty-hour weeks to taking full days off to drive him to doctor appointments where I'd sit and wait for him even though he always assured me it wasn't necessary. I had gone from taking random days off here and there to taking a "vacation" to prepare myself for his death. I had gone from taking a "vacation" to spending every spare moment of my day by his side or on my way to him. Tending to my father's last days had become normal. And then what? Certainly there could be nothing close to the normal I knew where my father existed in it, dying or not. No, normal as I knew it would not do.

I would have to find a new normal.

Day 7

The business of my father's death.

They were so "somber" with their "heartfelt" smiles. I felt an air of pity swirl through the room and smack me in the face as the receptionist led me into a consultation room. She offered me a three-ring binder to look through while I waited. Later I would see pity in the eyes of the mortician/caretaker/salesman (or whatever you call the guy who shows you the funeral options and caskets), and I would feel as if I was just another customer. As if I didn't matter, as if they were just pretending I mattered until they got my business. The business of my father's death.

I flipped through glossy catalog pages chock full of caskets. *Don't restaurants give you a menu while you wait so they can get you in and out quickly for more revenue?* Thinking about my father's death in terms of revenue made me glad I hadn't eaten more for breakfast.

I felt as if my father didn't matter to them—not until he was dead. And in the meantime they were just there to offer a service—a "nice" service, albeit—and it didn't matter what that service was, just as long as I could pick it out of a catalog and then be on my way. I sat in a waiting room for too long, and it had only been a few minutes.

I closed the catalog of caskets and pulled out the journal I'd carried with me to keep notes during the consultation, and wrote words that hardly matter now:

> I can't believe I'm sitting here. I knew it would come, but how is it already here? I just want him to have some peace. God, I must be horrible. I'm his daughter and I want him to die. The seizures have been getting worse. Probably having strokes. I don't know what to do. There's nothing to do. Nothing I can do. I feel so helpless. Even more helpless than he is. He's not even coherent any—

A cell phone rang. I lifted my head and saw that I was the only one in the room. It was my phone. It was Rick. I answered. He was at the hospital. Didn't look good. Twelve to twenty-four hours left. Doctors wanted us to say final good-byes. Final. Good. Byes. Final. I stared at my journal. Unfinished, pen still in hand. I set the pen in the crease between the two open pages and closed the journal. I got up and scanned the room. *What am I looking for?* Final good-byes.

A man walked into the tiny consultation room. He greeted me with his name, a consoling smile, and his hand, held out for me to shake. I reached out my hand but I did not shake his. I pulled my hand back and told him I was sorry but I had to leave. I told him my father was dying and I'd just gotten a call. He pulled something from his breast pocket. He put his business card into my hand and told me to call him if I need anything. His gesture seemed oddly cold, but I took his card and I walked out of the room. I put my sunglasses on. I walked outside. It was raining. I kept my sunglasses on and put my face towards the ground. I tried to be invisible. My tears were masked as rain walked me to my car.

Rain fell on my head, my sunglasses, my nose, but I didn't walk faster. I lifted my head and saw the cemetery across the driveway as I used the keyless entry to unlock my car. *My mother is just over there.* She was in the Mausoleum of the Resurrection. *"Resurrection" is the wrong word.* It had been years since I'd come there to see my mother's niche. I didn't feel her there. *She must not be here today. Maybe she's with my father. Maybe she'll greet him.*

The car door was open and I'd been standing in the rain thinking about my mother and this business of her greeting my father on the other side. *How long have I been standing here?* I got in the car. I closed the door. I cried. I started the car. I began to sob. I leaned my head on the steering wheel and I sobbed. As quickly as it started, the sobbing ceased and I wiped my face. I put the car in gear and I drove to the hospital.

I called Reese on the way. I told her my father would die today. I told her I was on my way to say my final good-byes. My throat tightened; my chest felt ready to burst; my heart, as if it were pumping broken glass through my veins. I kept my tears silent. *Now is not the time for an outburst.* I drove and talked and listened and waited. There was no time for a burst. Reese was sorry, but what could she say? She could not change it and she could not make it better. She said something but I didn't hear her. I told her I would be okay, that I'd be fine. I told her I would call her later. I hung up the phone. I whispered, "I love you." I sobbed. Again.

My car was stopped in front of the hospital. I didn't remember driving there. I turned the car off and removed the key from the ignition. I stared at the steering wheel, then out at the rain. The drops melted into the windshield. The wipers were frozen in mid wipe.

I took a deep breath. Then another. I heard a melody in my head. Tom Petty played between my ears: . . . *and the wai—ting is the hardest part* . . . I heard this on repeat like a broken record: *the wai—ting is the hardest part . . . the wai—ting is the hardest part . . . the wai—ting is the hardest part . . . the wai—ting is the hardest part.* The melody drifted away.

I took another deep breath before I got out of the car and into the rain. No umbrella. I stood in front of my car and looked both ways for cars. *What if I wait for a car and just walk in front of it?* I saw a car in the distance. Rain fell on me, on my head, soaked my clothes as I stood in the street, between parked cars. The headlights spotlighted the rain rushing almost sideways toward the ground. The car got closer. I braced myself against the wind. I could not move myself. The car passed me without incident, but I didn't wait for another car. I stepped across the empty street and made my way to the inside of the hospital. There were people waiting in the lobby. There were people waiting at the information desk. I passed both of these areas and pressed the elevator up button. I had all the information I needed. And I would do my waiting on the third floor. *The wai—ting is the hardest part . . .*

Back to business.

I chose a mortuary from the Yellow Pages I found in the waiting room on the third floor. I called and set up an appointment for that afternoon. *I just can't do this alone.* I asked Johnny to go with me and he did.

I walked through the front door, Johnny behind me. The woman I spoke to on the phone greeted us and asked us to sit. Pity did not circulate around the room as she showed us a catalog, and this surprised me. She seemed genuinely compassionate, and still this was business. We looked through her catalog of caskets—fancy caskets with ivory and marble and platinum and shiny gold options with bars and curls and pillows of lace and fluff—and they were too fancy for my father. A simple man, he didn't want all our money spent on a fancy casket and flowers.

We chose a pine casket, simple in design. An orthodox Jewish casket, all wood, no metal. And no Star of David because my father was not Jewish. He was a carpenter and would appreciate the craftsmanship of such a simple wood casket. He lived his life the way he would be buried. No frills. Nothing he didn't need. The casket didn't have to be fancy to do its job well.

I picked out a wood-bound sign-in book for guests. I chose an arrangement of flowers that didn't seem overbearing, even though my father did not want flowers. The flowers weren't for him; they were for the people who would think we didn't care if we didn't get them. This didn't make sense to me, but I chose the flowers anyway. *How do flowers show I care when they die in two weeks?* Maybe it meant life was precious and we should cherish it while it's here. Maybe it took our minds off reality for a moment. Or maybe it didn't mean anything at all. Maybe they were just pretty.

The woman pulled out a form. She asked us for the information that would go on my father's death certificate. We gave her names and dates and doctor and hospital information. She asked for his occupation. We said that he was a self-employed handy man.

This would not do. She wanted it to sound . . . better. She asked if she could put down "Home Restoration." I felt odd that even a death certificate required upgrading. We allowed her to use the phrase that made her happy.

The woman told us we couldn't pay for anything yet. We couldn't pay until they had provided services. Services my father needed to be dead in order to receive. The casket. The refrigeration. (I chose no embalming. We would display a photo rather than the man the cancer had turned my father into.) Three off-duty police officers to lead cars from the church to the burial site. The military burial procedures of the flag folding and playing of "Taps." All those things awaited my father's death and could not be paid for until it had happened, said the woman across the table. Services yet to be rendered.

I silently wondered if my father had died while we'd been away. And, somewhere else, I planned a funeral so grand that my father would be too uncomfortable to attend, too humble to comprehend he deserved the honor.

There weren't enough chairs for everyone who had come to visit, and the hospital wouldn't allow us to move chairs from another room into my father's. There was a rule that at least two chairs be in every room, whether the room was occupied or not, which meant that the nurses couldn't allow us to take even one chair from another empty room. I pretended this didn't infuriate me and stood, instead, while short-term visitors came and went.

I talked with people who had known my father for longer than I'd been alive. My father's best friend from junior high school, a forty-year friendship; members of a car club from high school, two years shy of a forty-year friendship; my father's best friend in adulthood and her husband, thirty-plus-year friendships. Friendships held for longer than I'd been alive.

Roy had raced back from picking up a new motorcycle in Texas and showed up the night before, pizza in hand. I had not seen him in fifteen years, but he looked the same: jeans, chaps, and a jean jacket, with his curly, wind-tangled hair harnessed in the back by a ponytail. He was unshaven, unshowered, unrested.

To me, after setting down the pizza: "You're all fuckin' growed up!"

Roy and my father were living together when my parents met. As the self-designated storyteller, he told me he was certain I had been conceived in the back bedroom of that little house they rented in North Hollywood. Roy detailed the house for me, telling me who was in which room, describing the hallways with details he probably made up, and how, even though the house was full, when Rick needed a place to stay when he got out of high school, they made room for him. And then there was the story of my father running marijuana up to San Francisco once when he was on leave from the navy.

My father? The devout Christian man?

I knew that my father smoked pot every now and then when I was a kid because I saw him do it once when we were camping with his softball team. Back then it didn't occur to me that it may not have been a one-time thing. Back then I still operated under the well-known house rule that one doesn't speak of what one sees, especially when it's uncomfortable.

As Roy spoke, the morphine dripped and began to make its mark on my father's movements. He shifted uncomfortably in his bed with each turn of the story that revealed what my father now likely saw as an un-Christian act: Roy asking him to take a package upstate. My father accepting. The apartment getting raided. My father simply being a part of the process. This was a part of his life for which he was ashamed—that shame was written all over his face; we could see it despite the oxygen mask and morphine.

For a brief moment I felt anger rise in my chest that my father hadn't shared these stories with me. By sheer nature of our father/daughter relationship, he got to know and love me with all my faults and flaws—but I had been allowed to see only what he perceived as his strengths. Now the truth was here, dancing right in front of me while my father lay mute via feeding tube and oxygen mask, morphine and cancer.

The moment I remembered the cancer I felt obligated to send anger to the waiting room. Regret took its place, and I longed for our Sunday afternoons of conversation. I'd replace our meaningless chatter of baseball and cats with curiosity about who my father had been before I met him. I'd ask him questions about his time in the navy. I'd ask him about his path to Christianity. I'd ask him about his relationship with my mom and how he handled her death. I'd want to know the whole him, and in return, I'd share the whole me.

In my head I could go back to the past and ask all the questions I wanted to, but it wouldn't change the scene in front of me. I felt my anger beckon for return, and I longed to scream, *Fuck this silence!* and clear my quiet lungs of the soot left behind by conversations never had. But on that day, I would allow anger no return. Plenty of time for anger on January sixth.

We had In-N-Out Burgers for lunch in the hospital room. Seems like burgers would be the least important thing to remember about all my time in that hospital, but there they are, stuck in my head. We sat in a hospital room around my father while he was not conscious and ate our burgers. We licked our fingers of cheese and spread, and drank our sodas and shakes. We then ate our fries, licked the salt off our fingers, and even had conversation in spite of ourselves.

It was nice to feel normal. Eating burgers and talking and laughing and licking our fingers seemed "normal," while, at the same time, we were in a state of hollow despair. It's amazing what you can block out when you're not even trying.

I can imagine what that must have looked like from the outside. A group of people sitting around a dying man, acting as if he wasn't dying, but eating comfort food and laughing instead.

Did I even look up to notice my father? I don't remember. Did anyone else? I don't remember. The whole thing is a blur. But I do remember my double-double with no onions and an extra order of fries. And I remember thinking afterward, *This is not normal.*

My father's father called. Thomas Reid. Tom. My grandfather, as it shows on paper. I never got to know him, and I'm not sure if that was my father not reaching out to him or Mr. Thomas Reid not reaching out to my father. I never knew him as Grandpa or Grandfather or Papa, so all the same I'll refer to him as Mr. Thomas Reid.

My father spent years wishing Mr. Thomas Reid would acknowledge him and love him just for who he was instead of being disappointed that my father wasn't Mr. Reid's son from his second marriage. Mr. Reid's son was a success. He went to school and graduated and then found a job in the profession he went to school for. He also had a wife and kids and a house and money and all the things my father felt a failure at. And Mr. Reid did nothing but stay away and allow my father to think that he didn't love my father for who he was. I pretended not to judge Mr. Thomas Reid for that, citing that I didn't know the man and therefore was in no position to make heads or tails of the relationship he and my father had—or didn't have.

Rick held the phone up to my father's ear while Mr. Thomas Reid spoke his words with my father unable to respond. I saw tears roll into and past his ears, down his neck. I don't know what words were spoken during those few short minutes. I can only hope they were healing words . . . that the tears my father shed were not of regret, but of relief and maybe even love.

The hospital visiting hours were from ten in the morning till eight in the evening. They also had a policy that only family members could stay the night.

But the nurses said nothing, and Johnny, Roy, Jon, and I talked until the early morning hours.

The Last Day

Bodies were scattered around the room by the time morning came. Both Johnny and Roy had taken to the floor, while Jon and I stayed in our chairs. Roy's legs and feet blocked the door, and Johnny's head was stationed at the foot of the bed, which made it difficult to maneuver myself over him without grabbing hold of the bed.

My father's face had all but shriveled away. His eyes were sunken into the sockets and bulging out at the same time. He hadn't opened his eyes or moved his body voluntarily since just after Roy made him cringe with his stories of the past. It felt as if he'd been lifeless for months, though.

I held my father's hand. Reese sat beside me. Jon sat beside Reese. Johnny sat the foot of the bed. Rick stood at my father's head and held his other hand. Then there was Roy, who paced back and forth for three or four minutes at a time. In between his bouts of pacing, he stood against the wall behind Rick and stared at my father, appearing to be in disbelief at the sight before his eyes.

We left the room only to eat or pee, and said little to each other in between.

There was a thickness in the air. Maybe it was just being in the hospital. Maybe it was the smoke-like dampness of the lung treatments my father had been getting.

I was surprised at the contrast between the unfamiliar coldness of his hand and the odd warmth of his forearm. I didn't want to think about it, but there it was: blood was no longer circulating to his extremities; it was only a matter of time before it stopped circulating all together. Cold hands, warm arms. Morphine circulating through his body on a mission to shut down every organ and take him quietly, peacefully to the other side. I felt as if I had injected my father with poison.

I never felt the final coldness of death on my father. I just felt it coming on. As I sat next to my father and held his hand, I remembered my mother's hands from fourteen years earlier. They had been cold. The kind of cold that can't be mistaken for anything other than death. I never realized it was so recognizable until I'd felt my grandmother's back nearly twelve years later.

Hands that didn't feel like hands and skin that didn't feel like skin. Sitting next to my father, I felt that chill creep down from his fingers, into his arm, and begin to take over the rest of his body. A whisper in my head: *You did this. If you hadn't started the morphine, he'd probably be fine right now.*

My mind was such a persistent liar.

Rick held my father's right hand with one hand and rested his other hand on my father's chest. "Please, brother, let go." Rick chanted this over and over, softly at first and slowly built it into a near roar. "Let go, brother. Please. Please, *brother, let go!* God is waiting for you!" Tears fell from Rick's eyes, rolled off his cheeks, off his beard, onto my father's arm. The air grew thicker with Rick's desire to see his brother finally at peace.

That's when I realized the thickness in the air was not guilt from starting the morphine drip, but simply our desire for my father's peace.

My father would take a breath and then seem to hold it forever. Forever. For . . . ever. And then all at once he'd let it out.

With every breath he took, we'd lose a little faith that he would take another one. And just when our faith was gone, and we believed that he wouldn't take another breath, one more would come. And Roy would pace. He'd stand still for a few minutes, lean himself up against a wall. One boot up on the wall behind him and one solid on the ground. And then he would watch.

My father's heart kept beating and his lungs kept breathing. I knew because my hand was on his chest; I could feel the beat . . . beat . . . beat . . . beat. And just when we thought he'd taken his last breath, his lungs filled with air, shallow and quick. Then all of a sudden my father's breath was replaced with Roy's exasperation: "That is one breathin' motherfucker!"

The room was suddenly full of laughter. Roy had said what we were all thinking, and put it in a way that none of us had the balls to do. It was just what we needed to release the tension.

After the laughter died down, I heard myself say, "Should we take the oxygen mask off?" I'd been wondering if the oxygen was keeping my father breathing. (How many different ways were there to take my father out of his life?) Rick spoke my wonder aloud and a quick glance around the room confirmed consensus to take the mask off. Without thinking about who would do it, I stood up, letting my father's hand go.

I reached for the mask and began to remove it with one hand, the other on my father's chest. The mask would not come off easily, and I had to use both hands to peel it from his face. It left an indentation around his nose and mouth where it had been clasped to his skin. His skin was sickly and pale and yellow and gray; he looked dead already, with his mouth naturally agape from the position of his head laid back on the pillow.

I held my father's hand again for a moment and placed my other hand on his heart.

This isn't like my mother's death at all, I thought, as I stroked my father's hair with my right hand while holding my left hand firm to his heart, afraid I wouldn't feel the last beat as it pulsed through his body.

Come to think of it, it had been seven days from the last time I saw my mother until I found out she was dead. And seven days from that time until I saw her in the mortuary. I held her hand—no, that's a lie. You can't say that you held someone's hand when the person is dead and doesn't know you're holding it, can you? I guess you can. It's just not the same when the hand you hold isn't holding yours back.

I entered the room. Was anyone with me? Must have been because I remember asking for some time alone with her. My grandmother was skeptical about leaving me alone with her. So was my father, but he didn't attempt to persuade me not to. They left the room, and a silence I'd never heard before filled the room. My mother was in the room, but there was no laughter. There were no jokes. No rules or restrictions. She wasn't ever going to ground me again or tell me to get off the phone again or tell me anything, ever again.

I had gone to a funeral with my mother when I was thirteen. This was nothing like that. I thought I was sad when Brandy Fernandez died. But if *that* was sadness, it felt nothing like *this*. I'd heard before that when you lose someone you love it feels as if your heart is being ripped out. I didn't believe that until I felt flesh tearing, my heart screaming, scraping from beneath my skin. It was slow and subtle at first, and then it felt as if chains and pulleys had been wrapped around each ventricle and were pulling my heart out of my chest. I was afraid to look for fear of seeing blood actually drip from my wounded soul.

Someone—who was it? My father? My therapist? A stranger walking down the street?—had suggested I write a letter to my mother and tell her all the things I wished I could have said to her before she died. To share my soul with her on paper, then read it aloud to her, to her spirit, as if she could hear it. I was told this would help me, would release guilts and angers and fears and regrets. I didn't really care what it would release; I just needed to focus on something other than my mother's lifeless body lying in the casket beside me.

Kneeling beside the casket, I breathed deeply to pull myself together and began reading. Childhood memories of moo cows and hill cows and pout birds that made me laugh. Birthdays and celebrations. One word and then another, until the sobbing started and I almost couldn't continue. I did my best to read through shallow, heaving breaths and told her I loved her in all my fumbling words. As the words leapt from the page to my tongue, and into the ether, their meaning seemed to dissipate. *If only she were here, right here, to hear me tell her I love her just one more time.*

I could feel myself missing her, aching for her in more than just my heart. I wanted to hold her hand again, to feel the warm touch of my mother's hand just one more time. In that moment, grief overtook my body, and I reached my hand into my mother's casket and put my hand on hers.

A pause. A silent movie of myself dropping my mother's hand, horror rippling over my face.

Her hand; it wasn't supposed to feel like *that!*

I remembered walking into the room just a few minutes prior, an image that's still stuck in my mind, nearly twenty years later.

Hair done up like she was ready for a party she never wanted to go to. Blue eye shadow looked out of place on the lids of her closed eyes. *What fucking picture did Grandma give them?* I wondered. Nothing looked liked her except her lips and her hands. Mostly her hands. I'd never noticed how much our hands looked alike until that day.

A brief touch revealed that they no longer felt alike.

I couldn't believe what I felt against my skin. Just like the silence I'd never known existed, I felt a coldness no living person can ever truly understand. For all of my sixteen years, my mother had had the warmest hands I'd ever felt.

They had comforted me while a doctor pulled thorns from my shins after I'd played a game of tag with a rose bush in the front yard. They'd brought me chicken soup when I was sick. Dried tears of sorrow and incomprehension with just a hug when she knew words would just not do. Those hands had cared for me more than I ever realized I would miss. And to touch them with no warmth, just ice seeping through her pores, stunned me.

I struggled to breathe for a moment and stood up, stumbling away from the casket. I dropped to my knees and sobbed. Loudly. I could think of nothing but the hole in my chest that I could feel but not see.

As I sat beside myself in grief I heard the door creak open behind me. I looked over my shoulder at the door and whoever was holding it open, and yelled what I thought was, "Get out!" It probably came off as a muffled shooing, but either way the door was shut and my mother and I and her casket were once again alone. I hung my head and returned to sobbing, although this time conscious of staying quiet. I was embarrassed at being unable to hold myself together, and didn't want any further disturbances. I quickly stood up, wiped tears and snot from my cheeks and lips and nose and chin, and knelt again beside the casket. I then quietly, in an almost inaudible whisper, continued the letter from where I'd left off before I'd distracted myself with my mother's hands.

After finishing the letter, I folded it back up and tucked it under her cold hands, leaving it to be cremated with her.

Looking back, I wish I'd kept a copy of that letter. At the time I'd been angry that my last moments with my mother had been disturbed, but I said nothing. Instead, I felt cheated and kept it to myself. The last mother-and-daughter moment I would ever have had been cut short, and there was nothing I could do to get it back. I sucked it up and went on with the rest of my life.

I would not be cheated out of my last father-daughter moment. Sitting beside my father as he fell further and further away from life, I didn't just want to feel his last breath, his last heartbeat; I *needed* to feel it.

A breath came and went, and his heart noticeably slowed. Then the second breath came, and his heartbeat was light and slow. We had learned to wait for the next breath, but no more breaths came. My own heart pounded as I felt my father's fade. I looked at Rick and back at my father and back at Rick and then my father.

Then I looked up at the clock on the wall: 6:08 pm. Roy had no exclamation to relieve us this time.

I stood and, for the first time, began to sob over my father's death.

When I finally came to a point where I could breathe normally and I felt I could speak a few words without cracking, I asked to have a moment alone with my father. The room cleared without a word, and I was alone with him for one last time.

I held onto the bed rail to keep from falling over as my knees gave out. I stood next to my father and sobbed for all that we were together, and all I would miss. I sobbed for all the love we'd shared, conversations we'd had, lies we'd told, truths we'd avoided, and circumstances we'd created for and with each other, which made our relationship possible.

I reached out and touched my father's arm one last time. Thinking I heard a whisper, I stood still for a moment. Nothing.

I placed my hand on his chest (to make sure the doctors got it right?) and then I turned away and left him.

The hospital handed me a short stack of paperwork to sign, I suppose to make my father's death official. Only the paperwork had a Mathilda Something-or-Other's name listed as the patient, rather than my father's. Unsure of exactly what it was I was signing, I asked a nurse if I had the right documents. She lifted her bifocals high on her nose and glanced down at the papers in front of me. Then, with a sheepish smile: "No, I'm sorry. I'll be right back."

I guess I wasn't the only one who'd had a long day.

After I signed the correct paperwork, we all walked like zombies to the elevators (which no longer seemed so pristine) and then to the parking lot. Most of us stopped at the edge of the parking lot to figure out our next move, while Rick continued on and walked to his car without a word. I didn't know where I wanted to be, but I knew I didn't want to be alone. Roy and Jon insisted we all needed a drink; Johnny opted to go home to his wife and kids while Jon, Roy, Reese, and I caravanned to a little Irish place in Burbank.

We were shocked at a full pub on a Wednesday night.

Sucked into my own world for the previous week, I had completely forgotten that the world went on around me, whether I chose to be a part of it or not. The USC Trojans were playing the Texas Longhorns in the national championship game, and all of southern California seemed to be out to watch.

The four of us fitted ourselves around a table for two and ordered a round of shots.

We simply toasted, "To Jerry," and put it down the hatch.

Given that I never graduated from college and didn't much follow college football, it's still strange to me that I know that the Longhorns beat the Trojans in a last-minute upset on January 4, 2006. Almost immediately after the game ended, USC fans filed out of the pub. The room became almost quiet upon their departure, and we ordered one more drink just to enjoy it.

In my head, Dave Matthews played:

> *Excuse me please one more drink*
> *Could you make it strong cause I don't need*
> *to think*[2]

At the end of our drinks we scattered, and I began searching for the new normal I'd been trying to put together since my father fell ill.

Important Distractions

My father's death and the days leading up to it were extremely distracting. I couldn't work. I couldn't think of anything other than my father or his cancer or how I would "deal" with it. Except when I would sit in my office and stare blankly at the walls. Everything I did seemed to be a waste of time.

I opened up my online journal account and wrote. I wrote what I was feeling, what I was amazed at not feeling, and sometimes I would just stare blankly at the screen. Sometimes I felt as if I had been writing for hours, yet when I looked up only a few minutes or seconds had passed. Other times it felt as if I'd been writing for just a few seconds and I'd look up to see that two hours had passed. Nothing on the screen. No work either completed or attempted. I honestly don't know if the reason I didn't get fired during that time was that I was productive enough in my up times, or if my employer was just gracious enough to turn a blind eye to my down times, given what I was going through.

What I was going through. I didn't even realize what I was going through half the time. At least, not while it was happening. It's only upon reflection that I can make any sense of it all, even now. All I could do at the time was put one foot in front of the other and live day to day, wondering what would come next. In the beginning I tried to predict how things would go, but I learned quickly that my expectations had no place on the path of my father's walk to death.

I expected my father to be coherent for another year, maybe two. That expectation was promptly blown out of the water. I expected my father to reject my homosexuality until his dying day. Blown out of the water. I expected my father to remain ever the same in my mind in life and in death. Blown firmly out of the water.

The distractions in my life while my father was dying were those of everyday life. Driving into work, watching a Dodger game with friends, sitting in traffic listening to music, working out with two ten-pound dumbbells every morning while I got ready for work, hiking on weekends or after work, reading magazines with lots of pictures, making love, watching endless reruns of *Friends* while trying fall asleep, playing softball every Monday night, and countless other mundane and meaningful daily goings on.

Given the hindsight of several years now, it turns out that many of the important things in my life while my father was dying were also many of those distractions.

Those were all the things that took care of me while I was away from my father so I could take care of him while I was with him. And while I was by my father's deathbed holding his hand, watching his lungs grasp for air, what was important to me was clearly my father.

When I was with him, there was nothing and no one else to focus on. When I wasn't with him, I had everything else to focus on, and thoughts of my father and his imminent death ran stealthily in the background of my mind like spyware. I had no idea the energy it took to focus on my father while he died. I assumed it was his energy his cancer sucked out. I assumed that supporting him just meant being by his side, and that being by his side would not take its toll.

I was wrong.

I had left Los Angeles thinking I was either deserting my father or running away from his cancer. I returned to Los Angeles thinking my trip had been a waste of time. It had lasted less than forty-eight hours having seemed to offer no reprieve from my father's condition.

Wrong again.

The single full day I spent away from my father wasn't a waste of time; neither was it a detraction of my love for him, but the source of energy I would need to make it through his last seven days.

Purpose of a Funeral

On the day of my father's funeral, Carolyn looked me straight in the eye and said, "This is a time to rejoice and celebrate your father going home to the Holy Father." I wanted to punch her in the face.

My father's death would be a learning experience—given some time to reflect and process my grief, perhaps—not a celebration before his body was put into the ground. Carolyn suggesting otherwise summoned the demons of a sorrowed heart, still reeling from decisions no daughter should ever have to make. I wanted to understand that she was coming from a good place, a kind place, and that she meant well, but instead I lashed out, screaming verbal atrocities of a trucker's mouth at her in the middle of the church as everyone stared on in disbelief. At least, that was the scene in my head. In real life, I didn't have the gumption to do anything but give her an odd, crooked smile and look away. *Well that's fucking great, but I miss him and I'm not happy he's dead. So save your rejoicing bullshit for someone who cares. Right now I miss my father and I wish I wasn't standing here at his funeral wondering how the fuck I'm going to get through it without falling completely apart.* I walked away, stewing at the thought of Carolyn's rejoicing, resentful of any suggestion that I ought to be feeling something other than grief over my father's death.

PUTTING THE PIECES TOGETHER

There were so many things I didn't want to do to start off my January. I didn't want to pick out a casket. I didn't want to pick out flowers or arrange the CHP escorts to get us from the church to Forest Lawn. I didn't want to sign the death certificate. I didn't want to sign the hospital papers. I didn't want to drive in the rain. I didn't want to see him in pain. I didn't want to choose a mortuary. I didn't want to pay for a funeral. I didn't want to contact the mortuary and say, "Okay, he's dead; you can set everything up now."

I didn't want to plan the reception after the funeral. I didn't want to go to the funeral. I didn't want to see the people who knew him before I was born. I didn't want to hear their stories. I didn't want to reconnect with people I hadn't seen in years, who might approach me saying, "I knew you when you were *this* big," or "You probably don't remember me but . . ." I didn't want to see my ex fiancé. I didn't want to do any of that. Because all of that meant my father was dead. And I wanted no part of that.

But I didn't get to decide what did or didn't happen. I just did what I was supposed to do. I reacted to things that happened around me because I needed to. It was expected of me to be strong. By friends. By family. Hell, even by me. I wouldn't allow myself to fall apart or to be weak while my father was alive. I needed to be strong for him. Not so that he could survive, but so that he could die in peace knowing that his daughter was strong. Knowing that his daughter would be okay without him. Even in the midst of his death I couldn't just show him who I was.

But maybe I did show who I was. Maybe I really am this strong. Maybe I really am this person I am.

RELATIONSHIP TRUTHS

I used my father's imminent death to delay whatever was to be the outcome of my relationship with Reese.

I wanted to believe that, if she went through my father's death with me, the experience would create a bond that could never be broken and she would see that we were meant to be together.

What it did was drive us apart.

Reese seemed to go deeper into herself, keeping more of herself from me than she ever had before. Her reasons for this, only she knows. I don't judge her for those reasons anymore; I see them for what I believe them to be: self-preservation.

My father's death and the evolution of the whole process brought me back into my mother's death. I didn't even realize it was happening. I had a sense of self in that I saw myself as the girl who had no parents. I found an identity in this. I found myself thriving on the attention I got from people pitying me. I didn't want to be pitied. Except that I did. On the inside, that pity made me feel loved.

I felt loved when someone took notice of me. People noticed me when they saw my "strength" in handling my father's death. But I was doing it for him and not for me. I was doing it for anyone who would notice me, and not actually for me. For me, I was silent. For me, I was weak by way of appearing strong and being unspoken.

I did not speak out. I did not ask for help. I figured I could go it alone. I figured I knew how to deal with death because I'd done it so many times before. I figured it was all the same. My mother was gone and she never came back. This is perhaps the simplest and most difficult consequence of death for the mind to grasp. I knew I had to prepare for my father being gone and never coming back, and naively used my previous experience to guide me.

But it's different when you get to prepare. It's different when you can allow yourself to be consumed by the cancer that's eating someone alive. I was consumed. I believed my father's cancer gave me a sense of purpose. I believed that appearing strong for everyone around me would somehow do my father a great service.

It was my homage to him, my way of honoring him by being strong. Oh, look what a strong daughter he raised. Which was true, but not for the way I handled my father's death.

In the weeks after my father's actual death, I felt nothing. I felt as if I'd already processed everything there was to feel around his death. I didn't miss him. I went to my first softball game without him less than two weeks after his death. Just a week after his funeral. I went up to the plate and wanted to hit a home run in his honor.

I did not.

I got a single. I ended up scoring a run. I felt like a failure.

Somehow, whatever will be, will be. I wanted to believe my father was there with me that night I returned to softball without him. In reality, he's gone and never coming back. At least, not physically.

What's important is that I have memories of my father.

I've learned that I don't need pictures or clothes to remember the people I love. I have memories. This is my new normal.

We try to tell ourselves that our loved ones would want us to move on, to move forward, but that goes against what we secretly wish in our own hearts. We secretly wish that if we die, hundreds or thousands of people will be touched by our lives and therefore our deaths, and will grieve over our loss and miss us. We secretly want people to be in mourning over our death, and we believe the length of mourning and sorrow is in direct correlation to how much we loved the deceased. And when we hear someone say that our loved one would want us to move on, we know that it's bullshit. We know that there's a little piece of us that wants to feel loved by someone crying over our death. If we cry over someone's death, it means we loved him or her. If we don't, then we're callous and unfeeling; we have no love in our soul and didn't care about our loved one. And that's a bunch of bullshit, too.

What speaks to the way we felt about our loved ones isn't our reaction to the news of their death, but the way we brought ourselves to the relationship when they were alive.

I would like to say that I don't regret anything. In fact, I *have* said that. But as I sit here now I can tell you that it's a lie. I regret not talking to my father more openly, more honestly, before I learned of his terminal illness. My father ended up giving me seven beautiful days to learn from, and I wonder how many more days could have been, if I'd gotten off my ass and been more honest and authentic with him and in our conversations.

I wonder what would have happened if we'd had authentic conversations while he was on my couch on a random Sunday afternoon rather than on my grandparents' couch waiting for death.

I'll never know the answer to that, but maybe you will.

Epilogue

Part I

I wondered for years who would break the news of my father's death to me. It never occurred to me that he would be the one. Or that I would walk him through it. That I would watch his last breath heave into his chest and wait to see it slowly released. That I would feel the last beat of my father's heart with my own hand on his chest. It never occurred to me that I would cherish those moments, just as I'd learned to cherish the six words my father had used to tell me of my mother's death all those years ago.

My father loved me, of this I am sure. Not because he told me, but because he showed me. I am finally able to recognize the words, the six words, my father's soul spoke to me as I held my hand on his chest when he left my life.

It's your father. I'm dead, Dian.

Part II

I held a basket of white roses, a symbol of peace, for participants to place on the casket if they wanted to. I held the basket, and they paid their respects. They picked roses from the basket, paid their respects, and then laid the roses on the casket. I wanted to be the last one to place a rose on the casket. And so I was.

I took a rose from the basket, and then set the basket down. I walked to the head of the casket, where no one had laid a flower, and closed my eyes.

Go be in peace. I love you.

I laid the rose on the casket and then placed my hand on the pine box. I wept openly and loudly again for the last time that day. I walked away from my father's graveside, unable to watch the lowering of the casket into the ground.

Honestly, I don't know how anyone does it.

---

[1]   Moore, Thomas. <u>*Dark Nights of the Soul*</u>. New York: Penguin, 2005.

[2]   Dave Matthews Band. "Grace Is Gone." *Busted Stuff*. RCA, 2002. CD.